The War on Terror

The Plot to Rule the Middle East

CHRISTOPHER BOLLYN

Also by the same author:

Solving 9-11: The Deception that Changed the World

Solving 9-11: The Original Articles

Published in the USA by:
Christopher Bollyn
www.bollyn.com

ISBN 978-0-9853225-4-0

Library of Congress Control Number: 2017911143

Printed in the United States of America

Book and cover design by Darlene & Dan Swanson of Van-garde Imagery, Inc.
The King's Cross designed by Peggy Lee Mead
Cover photograph of Islamic door by Sascha R. Leylamian
Back cover photograph of author by Ann Capotosto

This book is dedicated to all those
whose lives have been impacted
by the War on Terror.

From secrecy and deception in high places: come home, America. From military spending so wasteful that it weakens our nation: come home, America... Come home to the affirmation that we have a dream. Come home to the conviction that we can move our country forward.

Sen. George McGovern, Democratic National Convention, July 14, 1972

Contents

There is no instance of a nation benefitting from prolonged warfare.

Sun Tzu, *The Art of War* (500 BC)

Preface

Although the terror attacks of 9/11 and the War on Terror are developments of immense historical importance they are also terribly misunderstood. The fact that the public is burdened with misinformation and ignorance about these momentous developments is by no means accidental. The political establishment and mainstream media have misled and deceived the public by design. The purpose of this book is educational as it is meant to help disabuse people of the deception that has been imposed on us all.

While the nation was still in shock we were given a fabricated story that blamed Islamist terrorists for 9/11. Rather than investigate the crime, the Bush administration declared the attacks to be an act of war and took the armed forces into Afghanistan under the pretext of fighting terrorism. The military response has since expanded into fourteen nations becoming America's longest and most expensive war.

The only way to resist the war that has been imposed on the nation by deceit is to increase public awareness. As the truth reaches more people the deception loses power. The aim of this book is to increase awareness by focusing on the origin and nature of the deception and the strategic plan behind it. This concise volume reveals who is involved in this plot, how it was planned over decades, and why it has been carried out.

Comprised of articles I have written about different aspects of the War on Terror the reader may find some repetition. Some of the articles that refer to a specific event are dated for the sake of clarity. To broaden the discussion, Alan Sabrosky, a veteran and military scholar, has written the foreword for the book. To include the voice of those who have suffered the most from the War on Terror, an American Muslim perspective has been provided by the Nation of Islam Research Group.

Armed with a better understanding of the dual deception of 9/11 and the War on Terror the reader will find it easier to cope with the artificial reality we have been living in since September 2001. When one grasps the truth about 9/11 the falseness of the wars waged under the pretext of fighting terrorism becomes apparent.

9/11 truth is the key to freeing ourselves from the war propaganda and deception that has been imposed on us. We need to realize that the controlled media, the most active promoter of the war agenda, will never address

9/11 truth. If we want to restore peace and prosperity for ourselves and our nation, we, the people, must start by raising awareness of the deception among the people around us.

Christopher Bollyn
July 26, 2017

Terror is theatre... Theatre's a con trick. Do you know what that means? Con trick? You've been deceived.

John Le Carré, *The Little Drummer Girl*, 1983

Foreword

By Alan Sabrosky

Christopher Bollyn has written a concise guide for the layman to understand the so-called "War on Terror," in whose name the United States and its assorted allies have devastated countries across the Middle East. It is that, but it is also much more.

First, the book provides a way for even informed readers to appreciate better the origins, evolution, and extent to which Israel has driven a process by which the United States and other countries have systematically destroyed Israel's enemies, at no cost to itself. As we have torn up or assailed a long list of countries – only Iran has not yet been openly attacked, with emphasis on "not yet" – Israel, on the other hand, has not contributed a soldier, plane, or spent a single shekel in this war, all the while consolidating its hold on the Palestinians and receiving ever greater amounts of aid and support from the United States. "Such a deal" would be an understatement.

Secondly, it articulates the de facto capture from within of the U.S. government by the mostly Jewish Neoconservatives, many of whom being dual Israeli citizens and all more or less openly professing "dual loyalty" to Israel and the United States – a form of political bigamy that is every bit as dishonest as marital bigamy, and which only thinly disguises the controlling allegiance all hold to Israel, their oaths notwithstanding. Coupled with their domination of the mainstream media these days – a domination which makes it almost impossible for most citizens to be even aware of what is happening – this is a historically unique phenomenon, a "fifth column" at a national level completely without precedent. I have seen in my own lifetime the U.S. go from a country in which presidents like Eisenhower and Kennedy could unhesitatingly oppose Israel, to one in which virtually every figure in both major parties is obliged for their own political (and personal?) survival to essentially pledge fealty to Israel. "What a country," as the saying goes.

And thirdly, Bollyn gives an excellent assessment of where we stand now in the War on Terror, and how it might end – if at all. And here I confess to being more pessimistic than him. Bollyn is still hopeful that President Donald Trump – despite his personal and familial connections to Israel – may yet pull back from the path, as presidential candidate Trump professed to want to do. I simply don't see that happening, and whether it is due to his own inclinations, to the influence within of his daughter Ivanka and his son-in-law Jared Kushner, or a simple preference to survive politically and personally, the wars of regime change continue apace.

One thing is clear. Unless the American people understand what has really been happening in this gruesome War on Terror, and why, and the role Israel has played in it, they can never act to change things substantially. Bollyn's concise but genuinely informative treatment would be an important contribution to that understanding. Read, think, and learn.

Alan Ned Sabrosky
July 2017

*Alan Ned Sabrosky (PhD, University of Michigan) is a ten-year Marine Corps veteran. He served two tours in Vietnam with the 1st Marine Division, and is a graduate (as a civilian) of the U.S. Army War College.

Educate and inform the whole mass of the people… They are the only sure reliance for the preservation of our liberty.

Thomas Jefferson, 1787

Introduction

Coping with Artificial Reality

While this book may not bring the War on Terror to an end, I hope it will help the reader to better understand and cope with the artificial reality we have been living under since September 11, 2001. Armed with a clear understanding of who is behind the deception and why it has been imposed on us the reader will be able to make sense of the scourge of terrorism that has branded our era and the wars that have been waged under the guise of fighting it. This awareness can only benefit the sanity of both the individual and the nation.

The terror attacks of 9/11 ushered in the Global War on Terror, an open-ended policy of military intervention led by the United States, and drastic changes in domestic policy. The U.S. military has fought several devastating wars since 9/11 and brought about regime change in at least a half-dozen nations across the Middle East. Today, the war effort is ongoing and increasing in scope. The United States is currently fighting in several nations, including Syria where U.S. forces have repeatedly attacked Syrian government forces fighting terrorism in their own country.

Domestically, a host of security measures have affected the way of life in America. The most conspicuous changes are seen at U.S. airports where intrusive security procedures make passengers feel as if they are suspected terrorists. Additional powers have been given to agencies of law enforcement and national security to police the citizenry and conduct secret surveillance operations.

The government sold us the Homeland Security measures that were foisted on the nation in the wake of the 9/11 attacks saying they were necessary for our security and meant to prevent a similar attack from happening again. Shocked by the terror spectacle of 9/11, the public generally accepted the government's rationale for the wars, its huge defense budgets and police-state procedures as being good for our security. This is the main reason there has been so little resistance from the public to what is now the longest war in U.S. history. People have accepted these drastic changes as part of our new reality while they try to make sense of an artificially imposed *Zeitgeist* fraught with fear, hatred, war, and violence.

What many people don't realize, however, is that all of the wars in the Middle East and domestic security measures are based on an unproven explanation of what happened on 9/11, and most importantly, a false narrative about who was behind it. The official story blames Osama bin Laden and Islamist terrorists for the attacks, but if the government explanation of what happened on 9/11 is false, as the evidence indicates, then we have been intentionally misled about the very basis of the War on Terror.

The seemingly explosive collapses of the Twin Towers is a good point to illustrate that the official story is unproven. The federal government commissioned an agency of the Department of Commerce to investigate how the towers fell. The result of this study, however, the *Final Report on the Collapse of the World Trade Center Towers* (NIST, September 2005), fails to explain how or why the towers fell. The report admits its shortcoming saying it does not "include the structural behavior of the tower" once "collapse became inevitable."

Since a steel-framed skyscraper has never before fallen due to fire there was nothing inevitable about the collapses of the Twin Towers. The NIST report is infamous for having ignored documented evidence of explosions in the towers and massive amounts of molten iron seen in television footage falling from the buildings before they collapsed and found under the rubble weeks afterwards. Rather than explaining what really happened when the towers fell, the NIST report simply presents what it calls "a probable collapse sequence for each tower," which it explains in a footnote:

> The focus of the Investigation was on the sequence of events from the instant of aircraft impact to the initiation of collapse for each tower. For brevity in this report, this sequence is referred to as the "probable collapse sequence," although it does not actually include the structural behavior of the tower after the conditions for collapse initiation were reached and collapse became inevitable.

With the publication in 2009 of the scientific discovery of super-thermite in the dust of the destroyed Twin Towers, the government's explanation of the key events of 9/11 lost all credibility. Rather than address the published discovery of a highly energetic nanocomposite of thermite found in the dust, evidence proving that explosive demolitions destroyed the Twin Towers in which some 2,600 people were trapped, the Obama administration simply ignored the findings. Instead of addressing the evidence, President Obama increased the war effort in Afghanistan proving that the official story of 9/11 was created for the purpose of taking the nation to war.

This means the government and media have conspired to deceive the people about what really happened in order that the public would acquiesce to an artificial reality and an aggressive war agenda that were foisted on the nation based on a false narrative about 9/11. The fact that the War on Terror and key elements of the new security state, such as the USA PATRIOT Act, had been prepared in advance and were hastily put into operation indicates that these policy changes were the real reasons the 9/11 attacks were carried out.

It's not as though the terrorism of 9/11 simply fell out of the clear blue sky and the government then crafted its response. Rather, as I point out in this book, the War on Terror had been planned decades in advance and was simply made operational by the terror attacks. Starting their long-planned war agenda in the Middle East was the primary goal for the real culprits behind the terrorism of 9/11. The fact that the government declared the terror atrocity to be "an act of war" effectively precluded a proper criminal investigation by rendering war as the chosen option to deliver justice.

Understanding that we have been deceived by our government and the mainstream media about 9/11 and the War on Terror may not be easy for some people because it opens up a whole new set of suspected culprits to be dealt with. Denial is the most common response from people who find themselves unable to deal with these facts and revelations.

Examining the material presented in this book should be a liberating and empowering experience as one grasps the essential facts which will hopefully disabuse the reader of a painful deception. It should come as a relief to realize that the artificial reality that has been imposed on us in the wake of 9/11, in which fear is the main element, is simply not real. The threat of Islamic terrorism is a fear perpetuated by the culprits and is largely exaggerated. "Radical Islamic terrorism" is about as real as the myth of Osama bin Laden being behind the terror attacks of 9/11.

To comprehend the dual deception of 9/11 and the War on Terror is to realize that things are not nearly as bad as the government and media would have us believe. Understanding the fraudulent nature of both 9/11 and the War on Terror will enable you to overcome the anxieties that accompany the false narrative and to find balance and peace of mind in these turbulent times. Grasping the essence of the master plan behind the War on Terror will certainly change a person's perspective. It will give relief to victims of this frightful deception by giving them a bird's eye view of the massive web of deceit.

This handbook on the fraudulent War on Terror explains who is behind the war and why it is being waged. It is, of course, not truly a war against terror but a war of terror in which terrorism is the primary tactic employed in what is really a disguised war of aggression and conquest. To comprehend the fundamental deception behind the War on Terror is the essential first step to ending this global fraud. Awareness of the evil deception will bring the war to an end in the hearts and minds of those who grasp the truth. When this awareness reaches a critical mass, the deception will lose its power and the world will be relieved from the dark cloud of terrorism and war that has afflicted us since 9/11.

This crusade – this war on terrorism –
is going to take a while.

President George W. Bush, September 16, 2001

Chapter I

What is the War on Terror?

Any discussion of the War on Terror, also known as the Global War on Terrorism, is bound to be confusing. This is partly because the terms themselves are vague. Exactly what does it mean to wage a war against terrorism?

The War on Terror refers to the U.S.-led military campaign that began in the aftermath of the terror attacks of September 11, 2001. Rather than initiating a blue-ribbon investigation of the 9/11 atrocity, the administration of George W. Bush declared the attacks to have been "an act of war." This meant that instead of conducting a thorough criminal investigation and prosecution of the criminals behind the attacks in a court of law, it was simply left for the military to deliver "justice" to those the president "determined" had "planned, authorized, committed, or aided the terrorist attacks."

One week following the attacks that shocked the nation, the U.S. Congress passed, without objection, a bill into law entitled, "Authorization for Use of Military Force" (AUMF).

The essence of the AUMF bill says:

> That the President is authorized to use all necessary and appropriate force against those nations, organizations, or persons he determines planned, authorized, committed, or aided the terrorist attacks that occurred on September 11, 2001, or harbored such organizations or persons, in order to prevent any future acts of international terrorism against the United States by such nations, organizations or persons.

By authorizing the president "to use all necessary and appropriate force" against whomever "he determines planned, authorized, committed, or aided the terrorist attacks" without carrying out a proper criminal investigation left the door wide open for abuse and a wide-ranging war that could last for decades, as Bush administration officials suggested was the plan from the beginning.

In the years since 9/11 this is exactly what the War on Terror has brought us. The first military intervention began in Afghanistan in October 2001, an invasion that was decided by the White House on 9/11. Since then the authority given to the president by the AUMF has been used for major military operations in Pakistan, Iraq, Somalia, Yemen, Libya, and Syria.

Having been sustained for more than a decade and a half by two presidents, the War on Terror is America's longest war and is still being waged by President Donald Trump in all of these nations, and others. The current foe is something called Islamic State (IS, ISIL, ISIS, or Daesh) and military operations against this organization are ongoing in Afghanistan, Iraq, Somalia, Syria, and The Philippines.

Although the U.S. military operations in these nations have been carried out under the pretext of fighting the War on Terror, no evidence has ever been presented in the years since 9/11 proving that any of these nations were involved in the terror attacks of 9/11 in any way. So, what we see is a disguised war agenda being waged across the Middle East and beyond under the guise of fighting terrorism. The War on Terror is simply a cover for a much larger military operation to overthrow governments and redraw the map of the entire region. But this is not, nor has it ever been a policy of the U.S. government, so exactly whose policy is it?

What happened on 9/11 is that we didn't have a strategy, we didn't have bipartisan agreement, we didn't have American understanding of it, and we had instead a policy coup in this country – a coup – a policy coup. Some hard-nose people took over the direction of American policy and they never bothered to inform the rest of us ...

Whether you're a Democrat or a Republican, if you're an American you ought to be concerned about the strategy of the United States in this region. What is our aim? What is our purpose? Why are we there? Why are Americans dying in this region?

That is the issue.

General Wesley Kanne Clark, Commonwealth Club of California, San Francisco, October 3, 2007

Chapter II

9/11 Truth is Anything but Radical

The first signs of America's transformation after 9/11 were obvious: mass deportations, foreign invasions, legalizing torture, indefinite detention, and the suspension of the laws of war for terror suspects. Some of the grosser violations of democratic norms we only learned about later, like the web of government surveillance… Shocking policies abroad, like torture at Abu Ghraib and extrajudicial detention at Guantanamo Bay, today are reflected in policies at home, like for-profit prisons, roundups of immigrant children, and SWAT teams that rove through communities with Humvees and body armor. The global war on terror created an obsession with threats and fear – an obsession that has become so routine and institutionalized that it is the new normal.
– Thanassis Cambanis, "We are the war on terror, and the war on terror is us," *Boston Globe*, March 23, 2017

The "mainstream media" – a misnomer if ever there was one – would have us believe that 9/11 truth is the domain of radical and wacky "conspiracy theorists." These labels, however, are simply more misnomers used by the controlled media, which is complicit in the 9/11 cover-up, to misrepresent and marginalize the growing number of people who understand that we have been lied to about what really happened on 9/11.

The 9/11 truth movement is anything but radical. The real radicals are, in fact, the traitors in the political and media arenas who have pushed the lies about 9/11 and the War on Terror since September 2001. This distinction needs to be made absolutely clear.

In political terms, radical is defined as "in favor of thorough and complete political or social change." Conservative, on the other hand, is defined as "opposed to great or sudden social change."

The "transformation" of the United States with radical political and social changes began in the aftermath of 9/11 as a result of the government accepting and acting on an utterly unproven narrative about what happened on the day America was attacked.

The real radicals and revolutionaries are the ones who transformed America by taking the U.S. military into Afghanistan, Iraq, Libya, Somalia, and Syria, as part of the Global War on Terror after 9/11, without ever presenting any proof to justify going to war. The War on Terror campaign has robbed the U.S. of trillions of dollars, killed and wounded millions of people, and radically changed the way of life in America.

The 9/11 truth movement, which I have been a part of since the beginning, is strongly opposed to the War on Terror. This is because the truth movement is comprised of concerned and responsible citizens who grasp the essence of 9/11 truth. They understand that the War on Terror is based on a complete fabrication, known as the official 9/11 myth, which has been proven to be utterly false. In spite of abundant evidence disproving the false narrative, the controlled politicians and media continue to promote it. All of the drastic political and social changes that have been imposed on America and the world as a result of the 9/11 deception are based on nothing more than a pack of lies and fabrications.

TRAITORS vs PATRIOTS

It needs to be made crystal clear that the controlled media, which is complicit in the 9/11 cover-up, has shown that it is part of a criminal conspiracy by going on the offensive against the 9/11 truth movement. The truth movement is, after all, comprised of responsible, courageous, and patriotic citizens who stand by the sensible and logical demand to see the evidence before assigning blame and rushing to war. The people in the 9/11 truth movement have no reason to be ashamed, while those in government and media who have supported the criminal cover-up of 9/11 are guilty of no less than treason.

Treason is specifically defined in the U.S. Constitution: "Treason against the United States, shall consist only in levying War against them, or in adhering to their Enemies, giving them Aid and Comfort."

"Levying War" is defined as:

> The assembling of a body of men for the purpose of effecting by force a treasonable object; and all who perform any part however minute, or however remote from the scene of action, and who are leagued in the general conspiracy, are considered as engaged in levying war, within the meaning of the constitution.
> - *A Law Dictionary, Adapted to the Constitution and Laws of the United States*, John Bouvier (1856)

The U.S. government declared the 9/11 attacks to be "an act of war," which means that the people "who are leagued in the general conspiracy" have engaged in levying War against the United States. This would include those "who perform any part however minute, or however remote from the scene of action." This would also include those who participated in the 9/11 cover-up for they have given "aid and comfort" to those who carried out the attacks.

The traitors and radicals among us are those in positions of power in government and media who have used their influence to cover up the truth about 9/11 as they promoted an open-ended and illegal war agenda based on nothing but unfounded allegations. These people have no defense for their treasonous acts.

In the years since 9/11, we have lived in an artificially imposed reality where everything seems topsy-turvy, but don't let the professional liars in the media and government mislead you. There is nothing marginal nor radical about 9/11 truth. It is, in fact, the most important political issue of our time. It is also a common sense peace movement comprised of patriotic and responsible Americans who demand truth and justice and refuse to accept their nation being hijacked into criminal and costly wars of aggression waged on behalf of a foreign power. Truth-seekers should be proud of having the intelligence and moral courage to stand up for what is right.

In March, 1948, a Joint Chiefs of Staff paper on 'Force Requirements for Palestine,' anticipating the termination of the British Mandate, predicted that the 'Zionist strategy will seek to involve [the United States] in a continuously widening and deepening series of operations intended to secure maximum Jewish objectives.' The JCS listed the objectives as (a) initial Jewish sovereignty over a portion of Palestine, (b) acceptance by the great powers of the right to unlimited immigration, (c) the extension of Jewish sovereignty over all of Palestine, (d) the expansion of 'Eretz Israel' into Transjordan and into portions of Lebanon and Syria, and (e) the establishment of Jewish military and economic hegemony over the entire Middle East.

Stephen Green, *Taking Sides: America's Secret Relations with a Militant Israel*, 1984

Chapter III

The Dual Deception

The War on Terror, which began as a response to the terror attacks of September 11, 2001, is the longest war in U.S. history and probably also the least understood. It seems likely that there is a correlation between these two aspects of the war that began with the terror atrocity of 9/11. That is to say that one reason the war has dragged on so long is probably due to the fact that it is not understood by the public.

The War on Terror and 9/11 are like two sides of a counterfeit coin. If the American public had a good understanding of the false-flag deception of 9/11, then the fraudulent nature of the wars fought in its name would be equally obvious. Greater public awareness of the fraud behind these wars would naturally lead to growing numbers of concerned and responsible citizens demanding an end to the artificial, illegal, and extremely costly wars being waged in the name of fighting terrorism. However, because the two things are joined at the hip, a person who is confused about the origin and nature of the 9/11 atrocity is bound to be confused about the so-called War on Terror.

Since September 11, 2001, the U.S. government and controlled media have pushed a fabricated story blaming Osama bin Laden and his band of "Islamist terrorists" for the destruction of the World Trade Center and the huge loss of life on 9/11, without ever actually presenting any evidence to prove their case. President George W. Bush and his cabinet decided to wage war against Afghanistan on the night of 9/11 based on this unproven narrative, which has been parroted without question by the media. Likewise, the subsequent administrations of Barack Obama and Donald Trump have continued to support the utterly false 9/11 narrative and the war agenda it brought us.

Although evidence proving the falseness of the government and media story about 9/11 was readily apparent from the beginning, it was omitted from the media coverage that the public depended on to gain some understanding about the attack and who was behind it. By ignoring the evidence the pro-war media juggernaut simply rolled over the facts and those who used them to challenge to government's war policy in the Middle East.

Had the mainstream media functioned properly and reported the salient facts and observations that contradicted the official myth, such as the evidence of explosions and the presence of tons of molten metal in the Twin Towers and the dust thereof, the public would have had the information necessary to understand that they were being bamboozled into war. An honest discussion of the evidence by the media would have quickly revealed that 9/11 was a false-flag terror operation designed to be blamed on Osama bin Laden and Al Qaeda in order to start a long-planned and open-ended war in the Middle East.

Since 9/11 the mainstream media, controlled and consolidated as it is, has consistently spoken with one voice supporting the official myth about the terror attacks and the subsequent War on Terror. The average person, overwhelmed by the shock and awe of the 9/11 terror spectacle and conditioned to believe the government and mainstream media, was in no position to question or challenge the official story, which was designed to take the nation to war.

President George W. Bush spoke to the nation on September 20, 2001, saying:

> Al-Qaeda is to terror what the mafia is to
> crime. But its goal is not making money;
> its goal is remaking the world and impos-

ing its radical beliefs on people every-
where... The terrorists' directive com-
mands them to kill Christians and Jews,
to kill all Americans, and make no dis-
tinctions among military and civilians,
including women and children... Our
war on terror begins with al-Qaeda, but
it does not end there. It will not end until
every terrorist group of global reach has
been found, stopped, and defeated.

Nine days after 9/11, President Bush was preparing the
nation for an open-ended war that was evidently being
planned at the Pentagon to overthrow a series of Middle
Eastern nations. Six years later, General Wesley Clark described in a speech at the Commonwealth Club of California how he had learned in November 2001 about a
memo from the Secretary of Defense's office that called
for the U.S. military to "take out seven countries in five
years, starting with Iraq, and then Syria, Lebanon, Libya,
Somalia, Sudan and, finishing off, Iran."

The Pentagon memo to "take out seven countries
in five years" raises several questions of the utmost importance. Firstly, which came first? The plan to take
out seven countries in five years or the terror attacks of
9/11? And secondly, is this aggressive and criminal war

agenda in the Middle East in America's best interest, or is it really being waged for a foreign interest, on behalf of another nation?

It may come as a surprise to learn that the War on Terror doctrine goes back decades before 9/11 and is a product of Israeli military intelligence, not the Pentagon. Likewise, it was Ehud Barak, the former head of Israeli military intelligence, who appeared in the London studio of the BBC World television network just minutes after the planes struck the World Trade Center calling for the U.S. to launch "an operational, concrete, war against terror."

As a doctrine of Israeli military intelligence that has been promoted by Benjamin Netanyahu since the late 1970s in a series of books and articles, there is no disputing the fact that the War on Terror is a Zionist construct. Netanyahu and his father working under Prime Minister Menachem Begin, the self-proclaimed "Father of Terrorism," arranged an international conference on terrorism in Jerusalem in July 1979. The Jerusalem Conference began a "propaganda offensive to promote and exploit the issue of international terrorism," as Philip Paull wrote in his 1982 thesis on the conference, *International Terrorism: The Propaganda War.*

The Global War on Terror, which began after 9/11, is the implementation of the Israeli doctrine advocated by Benjamin Netanyahu since the late 1970s. While the war effort has radically changed the quality of life for Americans, it has not been a change for the better. With the U.S. military fighting and dying on an increasing number of fronts it is of the utmost importance that the American people clearly understand that these wars are part of a huge criminal fraud.

Just the war in Afghanistan is costing U.S. taxpayers $100 million per day (Source: National Priorities Project). As of September 2016 the Costs of War Project at Brown University estimated the total costs of the wars in Iraq, Afghanistan, Pakistan, and Syria, and Homeland Security from FY 2001–2016 at nearly $4.8 trillion (Source: Costs of War Project).

The terrorist masterminds behind 9/11 sold us a bill of goods, the fraudulent War on Terror, and we bought it – but we can't afford it. The costs of this open-ended criminal fraud will lead to national ruin. Americans urgently need to grasp the deception behind the fraudulent war, because we can only resist the war if we understand what it is.

With trillions of borrowed dollars spent waging futile and senseless wars in far-flung nations where there is no U.S. national interest, it would be hard to say that there has been any benefit to the American people to compensate for the trillions of dollars spent and thousands of lives ruined and lost.

In an Israeli newspaper article entitled "Report: Netanyahu Says 9/11 Terror Attacks Good for Israel," *Ha'aretz* reported on 16 April 2008 that Benjamin Netanyahu, the leader of the Likud party, told Israeli university students that the 9/11 terror attacks had been beneficial for Israel, saying, "We are benefiting from one thing, and that is the attack on the Twin Towers and Pentagon, and the American struggle in Iraq."

Well, if the War on Terror is an Israeli doctrine dating back to the 1970s to get the U.S. military to fight Israel's enemies, it seems we have answered the first question about which came first. The terror attacks of 9/11 did not bring us the war, rather it was the Israeli War on Terror project that brought us 9/11, a false-flag terror atrocity designed to make the Zionist war agenda "operational".

Secondly, if Benjamin Netanyahu, the Israeli prime minister and leading advocate of the War on Terror doctrine, tells Israelis they are "benefiting" from 9/11 and the "American struggle in Iraq" we have a clear answer to the second question about whose national interest is really being served by America's longest war, and it certainly is not ours.

Combining these facts about the War on Terror with those presented in my *Solving 9-11* set of books, in which I expose the Israeli role in the false-flag terror attacks and subsequent cover-up, it becomes quite obvious that 9/11 and the War on Terror are both products of Israeli military intelligence and that the terror atrocity was carried out to kick-start the Zionist war agenda.

This analysis, which is solely based on facts, is diametrically opposed to the interpretation of the War on Terror provided by the government and controlled media, which have been promoting this dual deception since 9/11.

This is why I decided to write a book about the War on Terror. We need to comprehend the nature of the deception that has been imposed on us in order to reclaim our reality. We cannot allow evil scoundrels to impose an artificial reality and false history on us and our nation. People who are deceived into war are not free people. A nation deceived is a nation enslaved. We cannot thrive as a nation if we are burdened with such an evil deception.

The War on Terror has destroyed thousands of lives as it has grossly perverted our thinking and plundered our national wealth. It is America's longest war yet there is virtually no resistance to it. I have written this book to help people understand the deception, because we can only resist the War on Terror if we understand what it is – in reality.

The Yinon Plan represents "the accurate and detailed plan of the present Zionist regime (of Sharon and Eitan in Menachem Begin's Likud) for the Middle East which is based on the division of the whole area into small states, and the dissolution of *all* the existing Arab states."

Israel Shahak, *The Zionist Plan for the Middle East*, June 1982

There is one thing that we do know. Oded Yinon's 1982 *Zionist Plan for the Middle East* is in large part taking shape. Is this pure coincidence? Was Yinon a gifted psychic? Perhaps! Alternatively, we in the West are victims of a long-held agenda not of our making and without doubt not in our interests.

Linda Heard, "Is the US Waging Israel's Wars?" *CounterPunch*, April 26, 2006

Chapter IV

The Yinon Plan

The idea that all the Arab states should be broken down, by Israel, into small units, occurs again and again in Israeli strategic thinking. For example, Ze'ev Schiff, the military correspondent of *Ha'aretz* (and probably the most knowledgeable in Israel, on this topic) writes about the "best" that can happen for Israeli interests in Iraq: "The dissolution of Iraq into a Shi'ite state, a Sunni state and the separation of the Kurdish part." Actually, this aspect of the plan is very old.

– Israel Shahak, *The Zionist Plan for the Middle East*, June 13, 1982

Iraq, rich in oil on the one hand and inter-
nally torn on the other, is guaranteed as
a candidate for Israel's targets. Its dissolution is even more important for us than
that of Syria. Iraq is stronger than Syria.
In the short run it is Iraqi power which
constitutes the greatest threat to Israel. An
Iraqi-Iranian war will tear Iraq apart and
cause its downfall at home even before
it is able to organize a struggle on a wide
front against us. Every kind of inter-Arab
confrontation will assist us in the short
run and will shorten the way to the more
important aim of breaking up Iraq into de-
nominations as in Syria and in Lebanon.
In Iraq, a division into provinces along
ethnic/religious lines as in Syria during
Ottoman times is possible. So, three (or
more) states will exist around the three
major cities: Basra, Baghdad and Mosul,
and Shi'ite areas in the south will sepa-
rate from the Sunni and Kurdish north.
– Oded Yinon, "A Strategy for Israel in the
Nineteen Eighties" *Kivunim, A Journal for
Judaism and Zionism*, World Zionist Organization, Jerusalem, February 1982

To understand why the United States is waging endless war in far-off nations across the Middle East, against people who pose little or no threat to the U.S., it is essential to understand that the operational plan being applied across the Middle East is something called the Yinon Plan.

This plan was written in 1982 by an Israeli strategist named Oded Yinon and published (in Hebrew) by the World Zionist Organization's Department of Information in Jerusalem.

Yinon's plan, entitled "A Strategy for Israel in the Nineteen Eighties" was then translated by Professor Israel Shahak of Hebrew University and published in English under the title *The Zionist Plan for the Middle East*. The Israeli plan calls for the destruction of the armies of the large Arab states and the Balkanization of their nations into ethnic mini-states, exactly as was done to Yugoslavia in the 1990s. Consider what U.S. intervention has done to the Arab nations of Iraq and Syria, and compare it with what the Israeli strategic plan called for in 1982:

> The Western front, which on the surface appears more problematic, is in fact less complicated than the Eastern front, in which most of the events that make the headlines have been taking place re-

cently. Lebanon's total dissolution into five provinces serves as a precedent for the entire Arab world including Egypt, Syria, Iraq, and the Arabian Peninsula, and is already following that track. The dissolution of Syria and Iraq later on into ethnically or religiously unique areas such as in Lebanon, is Israel's primary target on the Eastern front in the long run, while the dissolution of the military power of those states serves as the primary short term target. Syria will fall apart, in accordance with its ethnic and religious structure, into several states such as in present day Lebanon, so that there will be a Shi'ite Alawi state along its coast, a Sunni state in the Aleppo area, another Sunni state in Damascus hostile to its northern neighbor, and the Druzes who will set up a state, maybe even in our Golan, and certainly in the Hauran and in northern Jordan. This state of affairs will be the guarantee for peace and security in the area in the long run, and that aim is already within our reach today.

The Yinon plan "represents the accurate and detailed plan of the present Zionist regime (then Menachem Begin's Likud party) for the Middle East which is based on the division of the whole area into small states, and the dissolution of all the existing Arab states," Shahak wrote in his foreword to the translated article.

The Zionist vision for the Middle East rests on two essential premises: To survive, Israel must become an imperial regional power, and must effect the division of the whole area into small states by the dissolution of all existing Arab states.

"Ideally, we'd like to see Iraq disintegrate into a Shi'ite, Kurdish and Sunni community, each making war on the other," an Israeli official was quoted in the 26 July 1982 issue of *Newsweek*:

"The idea that all the Arab states should be broken down, by Israel, into small units, occurs again and again in Israeli strategic thinking," Shahak wrote. "For example, Ze'ev Schiff, the military correspondent for *Ha'aretz* wrote on June 2, 1982, about the 'best' that can happen for Israeli interests in Iraq: 'The dissolution of Iraq into a Shi'ite state, a Sunni state and the separation of the Kurdish part.'"

"The strong connection with Neo-Conservative thought in the USA is very prominent, especially in the author's notes," Shahak wrote. "But, while lip service is paid to the idea of the 'defense of the West' from Soviet power, the real aim of the author, and of the present Israeli establishment is clear: To make an Imperial Israel into a world power. In other words, the aim of Sharon is to deceive the Americans after he has deceived all the rest."

This is the real Zionist operational plan that the U.S. and its allies have been applying across the Middle East since 9/11. We are not fighting terror. We are re-drawing the map of the Middle East to suit Israel's strategic plan to dominate the entire region.

How does it feel, in the light of all that's going on, to be the father of terrorism in the Middle East?"

"In the Middle East?" he [Begin] bellowed, in his thick, cartoon accent. "In all the world!"

Menachem Begin to Russell Warren Howe, January 1974, *Washington Report on Middle East Affairs*, March 2009

Chapter V

The Common Origin

Although the terror attacks of September 11, 2001, have had a tremendous impact on world history, global society, and our way of life, the events that are commonly referred to as 9/11 are not well understood. What is most peculiar about 9/11 is that in spite of the huge effect it has had on modern history, the crime itself has not been properly investigated and examined as one would expect. The structural steel from the World Trade Center, for example, crucial evidence from the crime scene where some 2,700 people were killed, was hastily cut into small pieces and shipped to Asia. This indicates that the decision had been made at the highest level to destroy the evidence to prevent a proper investigation of the crime. The failure to investigate the 9/11 crime means that much of what passes for modern political history is nothing more than unfounded allegations and assumptions.

DECEIVED INTO WAR

A growing number of people who have examined the 9/11 evidence understand why the administration of George W. Bush allowed the evidence to be destroyed and why he delayed any inquest into the matter for more than a year. The evidence proves without a doubt that high-level officials of the government and owners of the major media networks conspired from the beginning to deceive the public about what really happened on 9/11. The purpose of the conspiracy was to promote a false narrative in order to take the United States and its allies into an open-ended and criminal war known as the Global War on Terror. Fifteen years later, both the conspiracy and the criminal wars it started are ongoing.

On the day of the atrocity, before a criminal investigation could even begin to examine the evidence, the Bush administration declared the terror attacks to be "an act of war" and that very evening the decision was made to go to war against Al Qaeda and the Taliban regime in Afghanistan. The haste with which the decision to go to war was made suggests it had been prepared prior to 9/11. By claiming the attacks were "an act of war" the government was relieved of having to present evidence in a court to prove that Osama Bin Laden was guilty.

So rather than carrying out a proper criminal investigation, the Federal Bureau of Investigation (FBI) was primarily engaged in confiscating and concealing crucial evidence to protect the official story. If 9/11 had been investigated as a crime, government prosecutors would have had to prove that Al Qaeda had the means, motive, and opportunity to commit the crime.

Rather than allowing the public to see the evidence and hear the results of a proper criminal investigation, the American population was immediately given a pre-pared, but wholly unproven, explanation that the deed had been planned and carried out by Osama Bin Laden hiding in a cave in Afghanistan. Less than three hours after the first plane hit, Ehud Barak, the former prime minister of Israel, chief of staff, and head of military in-telligence, appeared in the London studio of BBC World television and pinned the blame on Bin Laden. Although he provided no evidence to support his allegation, the Is-raeli military chief's conclusion that it was time to begin a global "war against terror" soon became the accepted interpretation of 9/11:

> The world will not be the same from to-
> day on, it's an attack against our whole
> civilization... If it is a kind of Bin Laden
> organization, and even if it's something
> else, I believe that this is the time to

> deploy a globally concerted effort led
> by the United States, the U.K., Europe,
> and Russia against all sources of terror,
> the same kind of struggle that our fore-
> fathers launched against the piracy on
> the high seas... It's time to launch an
> operational, concrete war against terror
> even if it takes certain pains from the
> routine activities of our normal society.

The same day, Ehud Barak appeared on Rupert Murdoch's Sky Television blaming Osama Bin Laden and ad-
vising Western governments to join a concerted effort to
combat terrorism:

> Most obviously my guess is a Bin Laden
> organization... The leadership of the
> world should be able to take action...
> Bin Laden sits in Afghanistan... We
> know where the terror sites are. It's time
> for action.

Nine days later, President George W. Bush told the
American people that Osama Bin Laden and nineteen Arabs had attacked the United States because "They hate our
freedoms." In the same speech, on September 20, 2001,
Bush laid out his plan to wage a global War on Terror:

> Our war on terror begins with Al Qaeda,
> but it does not end there. It will not end
> until every terrorist group of global reach
> has been found, stopped, and defeated…
> Americans should not expect one battle,
> but a lengthy campaign unlike any other
> we have ever seen… And we will pursue
> nations that provide aid or safe haven to
> terrorism. Every nation in every region
> now has a decision to make: Either you
> are with us or you are with the terrorists.

The haste with which the Bush administration took the nation to war in Afghanistan, without presenting any evidence to support its claim that Al Qaeda was actually behind the 9/11 terror atrocity, suggests that starting the War on Terror was the real purpose of the terror attacks. The fact that evidence from the crime scenes that contradicted the official narrative blaming Osama Bin Laden was being omitted from news reports seems to confirm this suspicion.

By leaving crucial evidence out of their reporting the controlled media has effectively protected the false narrative, the criminal wars, and the real terrorists from being exposed. Had the media presented and discussed all of the available evidence the public would have been aware

of the utter falsity of the government's story that was being used to take the nation to war.

CENSORED EVIDENCE

It was obvious from the very beginning that certain aspects of the 9/11 story were being censored by the media. Eyewitness reports of explosions at the World Trade
Center and news reports of the arrests of scores of Israeli
men who were apparently involved in the terror operation were among the stories that were reported once, and
never repeated. These omissions of important facts and
evidence from the media narrative indicated that a high-
level conspiracy involving the government and media
was afoot to sell the public a false story about 9/11 in
order to take the nation into "a war on terror… a lengthy
campaign unlike any other we have ever seen."

As President Bush promised, the War on Terror has
been a "lengthy campaign unlike any other." Fifteen years
later, the United States and its allies are still fighting two
wars that his administration started under the guise of
fighting terrorism. The wars and "homeland security"
measures that followed in the wake of 9/11 have cost the
United States more than $2.5 trillion dollars, according
to the National Priorities Project (NPP), all funds borrowed at interest.

One of the best indicators that 9/11 and the War on Terror are products of the same criminal conspiracy is the fact that the government and media continue to censor scientific evidence that disproves the 9/11 narrative, the false story that was used to take the nation into the open-ended military campaign. Indeed, when we examine the historical roots of the 9/11 atrocity and the War on Terror we find more indications that 9/11 and the War on Terror both originate from the same source.

The following are some of the most important forensic discoveries that have been completely omitted from the mainstream media reporting about the 9/11 atrocity.

MOLTEN IRON

Evidence of molten iron, the presence of which contradicts the narrative that the towers fell due to fire-induced structural failure, has never been reported or discussed in the mainstream media. A large amount of light-yellow and white-hot molten metal (i.e. 1100-1200 degrees C), presumed to be iron and obviously much hotter than burning jet fuel or an office fire, was seen falling from the 81st floor of the South Tower for seven minutes before the explosive demolition of the tower.

Firemen reported seeing "molten steel" running in the rubble like "lava in a volcano." Contractors also reported

finding "pools of molten steel" at the base of the eleva-
tor shafts of the three demolished skyscrapers (i.e. North
Tower, South Tower, and WTC 7) when they got down to
the bedrock of Manhattan, six basement levels below street
level – weeks after the attacks.

The clouds of hot dust that buried lower Manhattan
on 9/11 also contained molten iron in the form of billions of tiny micro-droplets of molten iron, called iron-
rich spheres. An independent survey of the dust in the
Deutsche Bank building on the southern edge of the
World Trade Center found that iron spheres comprised
nearly six percent of the mass of the dust ("WTC Dust
Signature Study: Composition and Morphology," R.J.
Lee Group, 2003).

A government-funded study of the dust published by
the U.S. Geological Survey (*Particle Atlas of World Trade
Center Dust*, 2005) contained micrographs of the iron-
rich spheres. The USGS survey also found tiny spheres
of molten molybdenum, which has a very high melting
point of 2,623 degrees C, or 4,753 degrees F. The micrographs of the molten molybdenum were not published
in the USGS report, but were obtained later through a
F.O.I.A. request.

The spheres of iron were evidently produced by a
highly energetic nano-composite of super-thermite,

chips of which were found in the dust by Dr. Steven E. Jones ("Active Thermitic Material Discovered in Dust from the 9/11 World Trade Center Catastrophe," *The Open Chemical Physics Journal*, 2009). When the bi-layered chips of this active thermitic material were heated to 430 degrees C, they ignited and produced extreme heat and iron-rich spheres identical to those found in the dust. Although this discovery, published in a peer-reviewed scientific journal in 2009, provides essential information about how the iron-rich spheres were created – and how the towers were demolished – it has never been discussed in the mainstream media in the United States.

PERSISTENT HOT SPOTS

Another important scientific discovery was made by analyzing the particles in the smoke that rose from the rubble in the weeks after 9/11. The smoke was found to contain large amounts of ultrafine particles.

Thomas A. Cahill is an expert on airborne aerosols and director of the DELTA Group at the University of California at Davis. In the days after 9/11, when he saw the light blue smoke rising from the rubble of the World Trade Center he knew the plumes contained large amounts of the very smallest particles, the extremely toxic ultrafine particles less than one-millionth of a meter in size, and smaller. Unlike the larger dust particles from the destruction of the Twin Towers, these ultrafine nano-size particles are particularly hazardous because of their extremely small size, which allows them to penetrate into the nucleus of the human cell where they wreak havoc on the human system.

The DELTA Group's research revealed the presence of these extremely small metallic aerosols in unprecedented amounts in the plumes rising from the World Trade Center rubble. Most of the particles in these plumes were in the category of the smallest ultrafine particles: from 0.26 to 0.09 microns. The extraordinarily high level of ultrafine aerosols was one of the most unusual aspects of the data, Dr. Cahill said. "Ultrafine particles require extremely high temperatures, namely the boiling point of the metal."

The data showing high levels of ultrafine particles in the smoke plume proves that incredibly intense hot spots, capable of boiling and vaporizing metals and other components from the debris, persisted beneath the rubble for many weeks after 9/11.

These important scientific discoveries have never been reported or discussed in the so-called "mainstream media." These significant findings have been omitted by the controlled press not because they lack importance, but because they disprove the official narrative of 9/11.

The fact that the government and media have protected their unproven myth for fifteen years indicates that they are actually both controlled by the same people who carried out 9/11 and deceived the public into supporting the fraudulent and criminal War on Terror.

The evidence indicates that 9/11 was a highly sophisticated false-flag military operation, a terror atrocity designed to inflict "shock and awe" on the public in order to instill fear and rage in their hearts. The purpose of the terror attacks was to compel U.S. public opinion to support an open-ended war agenda known as the Global War on Terror. If starting the War on Terror was indeed the primary reason for the false-flag terror attacks of 9/11, we need to understand who is behind the war agenda and where it comes from.

THE ISRAELI WAR ON TERROR

The War on Terror is basically an Israeli stratagem developed in the 1970s to deceive the American public into thinking that Israel's enemies are America's enemies. The purpose of this deception is to bring the U.S. military into the Middle East on a long-term basis to defend the Zionist state by waging war against its foes. The terrorist masterminds behind the War on Terror stratagem knew that a massive and spectacular act of terrorism would be required to trick the U.S. into fighting their enemies, so they began – evidently in the 1970s – planning the attack which befell the United States on September 11, 2001.

A timeline of some key events is helpful to understand the common origin and development of the 9/11 and War on Terror plots.

1977 – In a major turning point in Israel's political history, the Likud, a right-wing political coalition founded by the Zionist terrorist leader Menachem Begin (former head of the Irgun) comes to power in Israel ending three decades of Labor Party dominance. Begin is a notorious terrorist known for having ordered the bombing of the King David Hotel in July 1946, in which 91 people were killed, and the Deir Yassin massacre in April 1948.

1978 – Arnon Milchan, a top-level Israeli intelligence agent, produces his first movie, *The Medusa Touch*. The film's climactic scene depicts a Boeing 747 crashing into the Pan Am Building in New York City. Milchan was also responsible for illegally smuggling 800 krytrons – triggers for nuclear weapons – from the U.S. to Israel's Ministry of Defense between 1979 and 1983. Although his company, Milco International, was behind the smuggling operation, Milchan himself was not indicted.

1979, July – The War on Terror doctrine is rolled out onto the world stage in a well-planned propaganda offensive at the Jerusalem Conference on International

Terrorism. The conference is headed by the Israeli Prime Minister, Menachem Begin of the Likud. Begin's propaganda blitz is hosted by the Netanyahu Institute, an organization set up by Benjamin Netanyahu and his father for the purpose of promoting the War on Terror ideology.

"The conference organizers expect the event to initiate a major anti-terrorist offensive," Ian Black writes in the *Jerusalem Post* after the first day of the conference.

"The use of the military term 'offensive' is accurate," Philip Paull wrote in *International Terrorism: The Propaganda War*. "Four former chiefs of Israeli military intelligence participated in the conference: Gen. Chaim Herzog, Maj. Gen. Meir Amit, Lt. Gen. Aharon Yariv, and Maj. Gen. Shlomo Gazit."

The fact that four former chiefs of Israel's Directorate of Military Intelligence attended the three-day conference indicates that Israeli military intelligence was involved in the planning and preparation of this "propaganda offensive."

1979, September – Isser Harel, the former chief of Israeli intelligence, predicts with uncanny accuracy the events of 9/11 to Michael D. Evans, an American Zionist, saying Arab terrorists will attack the tallest building in New York City:

I sat with former Mossad chief Isser
Harel for a conversation about Arab terrorism. As he handed me a cup of hot tea
and a plate of cookies, I asked him, "Do
you think terrorism will come to America, and if so, where and why?"

Harel looked at his American visitor and
replied, "I fear it will come to you in America. America has the power, but not the
will, to fight terrorism. The terrorists have
the will, but not the power, to fight America – but all that could change with time.
Arab oil money buys more than tents."

As to the where, Harel continued,
"New York City is the symbol of freedom and capitalism. It's likely they
will strike the Empire State Building,
your tallest building [he mistakenly
thought] and a symbol of your power."
– "America the Target," *Jerusalem Post*,
September 30, 2001

1982, February – The Yinon Plan, "A Strategy for Israel
in the Nineteen Eighties" written by Oded Yinon, is pub-

lished by the World Zionist Organization (in Hebrew). Thanks to Professor Israel Shahak, the essay is translated and published in English under the title "The Zionist Plan for the Middle East." The Yinon Plan calls for "Balkanizing" the Arab states, i.e. breaking them up into ethnic enclaves, as was done to the former Yugoslavia in the 1990s.

"There is one thing that we do know," Middle East expert Linda S. Heard wrote in 2006, "Oded Yinon's 1982 'Zionist Plan for the Middle East' is in large part taking shape. Is this pure coincidence? Was Yinon a gifted psychic? Perhaps! Alternatively, we in the West are victims of a long-held agenda not of our making and without doubt not in our interests."

The Yinon Plan specifically calls for breaking up Syria and Iraq, which is exactly what happened to these nations after the U.S. military intervened.

As Oded Yinon wrote:

> The dissolution of Syria and Iraq later on into ethnically or religiously unique areas such as in Lebanon, is Israel's primary target on the Eastern front in the long run, while the dissolution of the military power of those states serves as the primary short term target.

1982, June – Under the leadership of Menachem Begin, Israel invades Lebanon with the intention of occupying the southern part of the country up to the Litani River, as per the Yinon Plan. The Israeli aggression results in the deaths of more than 20,000 Lebanese and Palestinian civilians.

1983 – Israeli military intelligence (AMAN), headed by Ehud Barak, begins arming and training the virulently anti-Western Hezb-i-Islami mujahedeen of Gulbuddin Hekmatyar in Pakistan. This operation is supported by U.S. Congressman Charlie Wilson and funded by the C.I.A. and Saudi Arabia. Israel provides the mujahedeen with weapons it has taken off the battlefield in Lebanon. Israeli military intelligence is creating the cadre of a radical "Islamist" terrorist foe to prepare the stage for U.S. military intervention in the Middle East. Hekmatyar and Osama Bin Laden begin working together in 1984 when Bin Laden's "Afghan Arabs" join forces with Hezb-i-Islami. Ali Mohamed, Bin Laden's first trainer, is a Hebrew-speaking Egyptian working for Israeli military intelligence. In 1994, these Israeli-armed and trained terrorist forces merge into Al Qaeda and the Taliban.

1986 – Benjamin Netanyahu publishes *Terrorism: How the West Can Win*, a collection of papers from a second Netanyahu Institute conference (Washington, D.C., 1984). The book is part of his continuous effort since

1979 to promote the doctrine of a global War on Terror with books, articles, and speeches.

1987 – Eight years after Israeli intelligence chief Isser Harel predicted that Arab terrorists would attack the tallest building in New York City, two of his veteran Mossad agents obtain the security contract for the World Trade Center and the Port Authority of New York and New Jersey. The Port Authority cancels the contract when it discovers that Avraham Shalom (Bendor), the head of Atwell Security of Tel Aviv, is using a fake name and has a conviction in Israel – as the former chief of the Shin Bet – for the murder of two Palestinians.

1993 – The World Trade Center is hit by a truck bomb in the North Tower, killing six people. Emad Salem, an FBI informant and critical witness is paid more than one million dollars for his testimony. Since the alleged conspiracy took place in New Jersey, the Israeli dual-national Michael Chertoff, serving as U.S. Attorney for the District of New Jersey, plays a key role in the prosecution. Chertoff's Israeli mother was one of the first Mossad agents. The media interpretation of the bombing leads Americans to believe that Muslims want to destroy the Twin Towers, exactly as Isser Harel predicted in 1980.

1998 – Philip Zelikow heads the Catastrophic Terrorism Study Group with Ashton Carter and John

Deutch. Their report is published in *Foreign Affairs* (CFR) at the end of the year. The Zelikow report begins by "imagining the transforming event" of catastrophic terrorism "that could happen next month." Ashton Carter and John Deutch are senior partners of Global Technology Partners, "an exclusive affiliate of Rothschild N.A., formed to make acquisitions of and investments in technology, defense, and aerospace-related companies." Zelikow, the head of the group, will go on to head the 9/11 Commission and write most of the commission's report. Carter goes on to become Secretary of Defense under President Obama.

2000 – Arnon Milchan and his business partner Rupert Murdoch produce a TV series called "The Lone Gunmen." The first episode of the series, "Pilot", is about a passenger airliner being remotely hijacked and flown into the World Trade Center. The footage for the climactic sequence when the plane is approaching the Twin Towers is actually filmed flying a helicopter over Manhattan. The program airs on Murdoch's Fox Television on March 4, 2001, six months before 9/11, and is viewed by 13 million U.S. viewers.

2000, September – A Neo-Con think tank, the Project for the New American Century (PNAC) founded by William Kristol and Robert Kagan in 1997, publishes a paper entitled "Rebuilding America's Defenses," which specifically calls for the U.S. to occupy Iraq and other radical changes in U.S. military policy. The "process of transformation" the paper says, "is likely to be a long one, absent some catastrophic and catalyzing event – like a new Pearl Harbor."

2001, 9/11 – In a spectacular act of terrorism the tallest buildings in New York City are destroyed, just as Mossad chief Isser Harel had predicted 22 years earlier. The terror attacks of 9/11 bear the hallmarks of an Israeli false-flag operation designed to start their long-planned war agenda. Ehud Barak immediately calls for an operational "war against terror" on BBC World and Sky News television. Barak is Israel's most senior military officer as the former commander of the Israel's covert commando force (Sayeret Matkal), head of military intelligence (AMAN), chief of staff, and both prime minister and defense minister until March 2001.

While tens of thousands are feared dead in the rubble, the *New York Times* asks Benjamin Netanyahu on 9/11 about the effect the terror attacks will have on U.S.-Israeli relations. Netanyahu says: "It's very good... it will generate immediate sympathy."

2001, October 7 – The War on Terror begins with a U.S. bombing campaign in Afghanistan. In December, the Taliban is ousted and Hamid Karzai is installed to head a transitional government. The war in Afghanistan goes on to become the longest war in U.S. history.

2001, October – General Wesley Clark visits the Pentagon and is informed of the planned war agenda: "We're going to take out seven countries in five years, starting with Iraq, and then Syria, Lebanon, Libya, Somalia, Sudan, and finishing off, Iran."

2003, March 20 – The Bush administration invades Iraq claiming that Saddam Hussein possesses weapons of mass destruction (WMDs) and that the Iraqi government poses an immediate threat to the United States and its coalition allies. No evidence, however, of WMDs is found to verify the claims used to start the war.

2003, March 31 – The 9/11 Commission headed by Executive Director Philip Zelikow holds its first hearing in New York City. Zelikow has a complete outline of the commission's final report before the commission even begins its work. His outline is detailed with chapter headings, subheadings, and sub-subheadings, as revealed by Philip Shenon in *The Commission: The Uncensored History of the 9/11 Investigation*. Zelikow shows his report to Commission Chairman Tom Kean and Vice chairman Lee Hamilton and they like it, but think it could be seen as evidence of having a pre-determined outcome. They decide to keep it secret from the commission's staff.

2008, April 16 – "Netanyahu Says 9/11 Terror Attacks Good for Israel" the Israeli newspaper *Ha'aretz* reports, quoting Benjamin Netanyahu: "We are benefiting from one thing, and that is the attack on the Twin Towers and Pentagon, and the American struggle in Iraq."

Although this timeline is by no means complete, it is sufficient to show the common origin of the 9/11 terror atrocity and the War on Terror. Both plots originated from the same source at the same time – Israeli military intelligence under the political leadership of the notorious terrorist Menachem Begin of the Likud (formerly Irgun) in the late 1970s. A closer examination of the evidence is found in *Solving 9/11: The Deception that Changed the World* and *Solving 9/11: The Original Articles*, a set of books containing my 9/11 research that shows exactly who had the means, motive, and opportunity to commit the crime – and carry out the cover-up upon which the War on Terror depended.

It is not, as the American people were led to believe, that the terrorism of 9/11 simply fell out of the clear blue sky and that the War on Terror and radical changes in U.S. domestic and foreign policy followed as a result. Rather, the evidence indicates that the 9/11 attacks were carried out in order to kick-start the pre-planned Israeli war agenda known as the War on Terror.

But in many cases, of course, it is perfectly possible to determine who the terrorists are and who stands behind them. If governments have failed to do this, it is more often not for lack of knowledge but for lack of courage and moral clarity.

Benjamin Netanyahu, *Terrorism: How the West Can Win* (1986)

Chapter VI

A Massive Criminal Fraud

May 23, 2013

The War on Terror is designed to rob and plunder the American republic. It has cost the United States more than $4 trillion at current best estimates. Nearly all of that money has been borrowed at interest. Understanding who is behind the War on Terror helps one comprehend the real perpetrators behind 9/11, and why they carried out the false-flag terror atrocity that changed America.

FAKE TERROR PLOTS

The FBI has set up many fake terror plots since 9/11. In an October 2011 article entitled "Government-Generated Plots," Andrew P. Napolitano, a former Superior Court Judge (NJ), explained:

> If you ask the leadership of the FBI… it
> will tell you that it has foiled about sev-
> enteen plots to kill Americans during

the past ten years... The seventeen that were interrupted by the feds were created by them... They all have a common and reprehensible thread. They were planned, plotted, controlled, and carried out by the federal government itself.

The first bombing of the World Trade Center in 1993 was apparently a similar operation with involvement by the FBI. In setting up the "terrorists" the FBI used Emad Salem, a former Egyptian army officer, who served as a highly-paid informant to help entrap the individuals charged with the crime.

After 9/11 the FBI, under the supervision of Asst. Attorney General Michael Chertoff, allowed crucial evidence from the crime scene, such as the structural steel, to be destroyed without being examined. Rather than properly investigating the crime the government blamed Osama Bin Laden without presenting evidence to prove its case. Bin Laden was convicted in the court of public opinion, which duly swung in favor of waging the War on Terror and invading both Afghanistan and Iraq.

BOSTON MARATHON BOMBING

The Boston Marathon bombing on April 15, 2013, is a bizarre case of what appears to be fake terrorism for which no organization claimed responsibility. Although the FBI says that Dzhokhar Tsarnaev, a 19-year-old Chechen Muslim immigrant, has admitted being involved, the confession was obtained before he had been read his Miranda rights. This is similar to the U.S. government claim that a Guantanamo detainee named Khalid Sheikh Mohammed has confessed to being the "mastermind of 9/11." Confessions like these, obtained through torture or coercion, are not valid evidence.

There are significant contradictions with the FBI account linking the Tsarnaev brothers to the crime. The day after the bombing, for example, Richard DesLauriers, FBI special agent in charge of the investigation, said "both of the explosives were placed in a dark-colored nylon bag or backpack." Video footage from the marathon, however, shows Dzhokhar carrying a light-colored backpack.

Like 9/11, the most suspicious thing about the Boston bombing is the lack of a logical motive. Terrorism is defined as the use of violence in the pursuit of political aims. With 9/11 and the Boston bombing there is no rational reason why anyone would commit such atrocities, except one: to falsely blame the heinous crime on a targeted group. This suggests that 9/11 and the Boston bombing are cases of false-flag terrorism designed to be blamed on Muslims.

The FBI had extensive contact with the older Tsarnaev, Tamarlan, according to his mother. Zubeidat Tsarnaeva said her son had been under constant FBI surveillance for years:

> He was controlled by FBI like for five – three, five years. They knew what my son was doing. They knew what actions and what the sites on Internet he was going. They used to come home, they used to come and talk to me. They used to tell me, you know, that they're controlling his – they were telling me that he is a really extremist leader and they are afraid of him.

The FBI contact with Tamarlan has led many to suspect that the Tsarnaev brothers have been framed. Given the history of government-generated plots there is good reason for such suspicion. But why is the FBI working to entrap Muslims? What purpose do these fake terror plots serve?

9/11 and the War on Terror have profoundly changed the way Americans live and how they view the world. The question is, do Americans face a real and genuine threat of terrorism or is it all a hoax designed to instill fear and manipulate public opinion to support U.S. military interventions in the Muslim world?

THE ISRAELI REACTION TO 9/11

Shortly after the towers were struck on 9/11, Ehud Barak, the former Israeli prime minister, appeared on BBC World, a television network watched by millions of people around the world, with his appeal for "an operational, concrete war against terror." On the same day, James Bennet of the *New York Times* asked Benjamin Netanyahu what the terror atrocity meant for relations between the United States and Israel. Netanyahu replied, "It's very good… Well, not very good, but it will generate immediate sympathy."

To understand the Israeli reaction to 9/11 we need to view the terror spectacle as a crucial part of a pre-planned Zionist construct known as the War on Terror. Netanyahu's odd remark makes sense when we consider that 9/11 is the keystone of an Israeli war strategy that Netanyahu has been pushing since 1979.

While most Americans view 9/11 as the beginning of the War on Terror, 9/11 is really the final piece, the keystone of a Zionist set-up that had been in development for more than two decades. The War on Terror doctrine was first introduced at an international conference organized by the Jonathan [Netanyahu] Institute in Jerusalem in July 1979.

Menachem Begin, the former Irgun leader who ordered the 1946 bombing of the King David Hotel, became prime minister in 1977. Two years later, Prime Minister Begin headed the committee that arranged the Jerusalem Conference on International Terrorism, an event designed "to launch an international propaganda offensive to promote and exploit the issue of international terrorism," according to Philip Paull's 1982 thesis *International Terrorism: The Propaganda War.*

"The propaganda 'blitz' originated in Jerusalem," Paull wrote. "The conspiratorial network included present and former members of the Israeli and United States governments," including George H.W. Bush, along with "seven hundred invited foreign journalists, influential friends of Israel, and top-ranking members of the Israeli military, diplomatic, and intelligence establishment."

"Using the Jerusalem Conference as a fulcrum, the Jonathan Institute fabricated and helped spread misinformation about the worldwide terrorist threat," Paull wrote. The Netanyahu institute was founded by Benjamin Netanyahu and his father, Benzion, the founding chairman. Benzion Netanyahu articulated the purpose of the conference in his opening speech: "This conference was called to serve as the beginning of a new process – the purpose of rallying the democracies of the world to a struggle against terrorism and the dangers it represents."

"This 'anti-terrorist' propaganda campaign was and is being conducted in a style reminiscent of wartime 'psychological warfare' by journalists serving as conduits and spreaders of misinformation originating in Jerusalem," Paull wrote. Spreading the propaganda from the Netanyahu institute began immediately in the mass media. Five days after the conference, the *International Herald Tribune* declared in its lead editorial, "The Issue is Terrorism." Echoing his father's call for a global war on terrorism, Benjamin Netanyahu wrote a series of books with titles like *International Terrorism: Challenge and Response, Fighting Terrorism,* and *Terrorism: How the West Can Win.*

ISRAELI PRESCIENCE OF 9/11

While Benjamin Netanyahu was pushing the propaganda campaign, a former head of Israeli intelligence was predicting a 9/11 type attack that would compel the United States to join Israel's pre-planned war against terror.

In 1979, Isser Harel, the veteran Israeli intelligence chief, predicted a terror attack like 9/11 to Michael D. Evans, an American Zionist activist. As Evans wrote, "My last question was would terrorism ever come to America. 'You have the power to fight it,' he said, 'but not the will. They have the will, but not the power. All of that will change in time. Yes, I fear it will come to New York and your tallest building, which is a symbol of your fertility.'"

Arnon Milchan, a senior Mossad operative who was later involved in the smuggling of nuclear trigger devices, made a film in 1978 that depicted how such an attack might occur. In Milchan's first movie, *The Medusa Touch*, an airliner flies into the Pan Am Building in New York City, exploding in a ball of fire. In 2000, Rupert Murdoch, Milchan's business partner, made *The Lone Gunmen*, a television film in which a remotely-controlled airliner was flown into the World Trade Center. To film the sequence of the plane flying toward the World Trade Center Murdoch's crew actually used a helicopter to fly the approach to the Twin Towers in 2000. It would be very interesting to know who was involved in the filming of this scene which became real six months after the film aired in March 2001. I would suspect that this filming was actually part of the final planning for the 9/11 attacks.

Milchan is called "LAKAM Agent No. 1" in an Israeli biography, *Confidential: The Life of Secret Agent Turned Hollywood Tycoon - Arnon Milchan.* LAKAM is an acronym for Bureau of Scientific Relations, an Israeli intelligence agency that collected scientific and technical intelligence abroad, particularly for Israel's nuclear program. In the 1980s, when Milchan was involved with Benjamin Netanyahu in the illegal smuggling of nuclear triggers, LAKAM was being run by the Israeli spy-master Rafi Eitan.

The coincidence of the Netanyahu conference, Isser Harel's uncanny prediction of what was to occur on 9/11, and Arnon Milchan's film depicting the terror spectacle that befell the World Trade Center indicates that such an attack was being discussed and visualized at the highest level of Israeli intelligence in the late 1970s. The fact that veteran Mossad officers who had worked with Isser Harel for decades obtained the security contract for the World Trade Center in 1987 suggests there was an Israeli conspiracy afoot to make the ideation of 9/11 become reality.

As I describe in "The Architecture of Terror," a chapter in my book *Solving 9/11: The Deception that Changed the World*, two veteran Israeli intelligence agents, Peter Zvi Malkin and Avraham Bendor (a.k.a. Avraham Shalom) obtained the security contract in 1987. The Port Authority of New York and New Jersey (PANYNJ), the

agency that owned the World Trade Center, had negoti-
ated the contract with a company called Atwell Security
of Tel Aviv. Bendor was the president of Atwell Security,
a company owned by Shaul Eisenberg, the China-based
senior Mossad operative.

On April 12, 1987, the *Washington Post* reported
that the Port Authority was canceling the contract with
Atwell Security:

> The authority that runs the three major
> airports in the New York City area is can-
> celing a $75,000 contract with an Israeli
> security company after learning that the
> firm is headed by an Israeli secret service
> chief forced to resign last year following
> disclosures that he had ordered murders
> of two Palestinian bus hijackers.

Zvi Malkin and Avraham Bendor had worked under
Rafi Eitan and Isser Harel, the chief of the Mossad, on
the kidnapping of Adolf Eichmann in Argentina in 1960.
Two years later, as Harel began a covert campaign to kill
German rocket scientists, he drafted operational units
from the Shin Bet, headed by Zvi Malkin and Rafi Eitan,
and one from the Mossad, headed by Yitzhak Shamir. In
Operation Damocles, which began in August 1962, the

Israeli agents working under Harel used letter bombs and kidnappings to kill German scientists and others.

Rafi Eitan and Avraham Bendor were also involved in the theft of a large amount of weapons-grade uranium in the United States in 1968. They traveled with two other Israeli agents to a nuclear plant in Apollo, Pennsylvania, from where large amounts of weapons-grade uranium disappeared and were diverted to Israel. This smuggling of weapons-grade uranium from the United States would have directly involved Shimon Peres, the godfather of Israel's nuclear arsenal.

Later, in 1985, the same group of agents was implicated in the smuggling of more than 800 nuclear triggers (krytrons) to Israel, using Arnon Milchan (the Mossad film maker) as the main connection and conduit for the smuggling. Benjamin Netanyahu worked for Milchan's company at the time. In the same year, the Israeli spy Jonathan Pollard was discovered working under Rafi Eitan.

Eitan has always considered the United States to be an enemy of Israel: "I failed in the Pollard affair, just as I failed in other intelligence operations beyond enemy lines," Eitan said in an interview with *Yediot Aharonot* in June 1997.

In all of these operations, including the attempt to obtain the security contract for the World Trade Center, the same small group of veteran Israeli terrorists/criminals is involved: Yitzhak Shamir, Shimon Peres, Isser Harel, Rafi Eitan, Peter Zvi Malkin, Avraham Bendor (Shalom), Shaul Eisenberg, Arnon Milchan, and Benjamin Netanyahu. Malkin and Bendor had officially retired when they tried to get the security contract, which was cancelled only after it was discovered that Bendor was using a false name and had been involved in the murder of Palestinians in 1984 while working as the head of Shin Bet under Prime Minister Yitzhak Shamir.

Shalom Bendor had been forced to resign as head of the Shin Bet in 1986 due to his role in the murder of two Palestinians by his agents. After failing to secure the Atwell security contract for the World Trade Center, Shalom went to work for Kroll Associates and Maurice Greenberg. Kroll Associates obtained the security contract for the World Trade Center in 1993 after the first bombing and was responsible for security at the WTC until 9/11.

Understanding the intellectual origins of the 9/11 plot and how it was essential to the realization of the Israeli strategy known as the War on Terror helps to clarify the real motive for the crime that changed the world.

Identifying the Israeli intelligence agents involved in the ideation and preparation of the 9/11 terror attacks exposes a small group of veteran Zionist criminals who have employed terrorism as a tool since the 1940s.

He [Pinhas Lavon] inspired and cultivated the negative adventuristic trend in the army and preached the doctrine that not the Arab countries but the Western Powers are the enemy, and the only way to deter them from their plots is through direct actions that will terrorize them…

Peres [Shimon] shares the same ideology [as Lavon]: he wants to frighten the West into supporting Israel's aims.

Moshe Sharett, Prime Minister of Israel (1954-1955)
"The Lavon Affair: Terrorism to Coerce the West"
Israel's Sacret Terrorism, Livia Rokach, AAUG Press, 1980

Chapter VII

Frighten the West: The Israeli Roots of Terrorism

November 22, 2015

The War on Terror is a massive fraud based on deception and illusion. As long as Western governments and societies allow themselves to be deceived about the true nature of terrorism, the war and the threat it is meant to eradicate will only get worse. For our political leaders and media to go along with false-flag deceptions and to flail away at phantoms is to ensure that the war will go on for a very long time. The only way to liberate ourselves and our nations from this madness is to expose the true source of terrorism.

So, here we are, fourteen years after 9/11, having waged two wars of aggression in which millions of lives have been ruined, having suffered the imposition of draconian "anti-terrorism" legislation, and having wasted trillions of borrowed dollars in the War on Terror – and still there is no end in sight.

In spite of all this effort and money spent, the threat of global terrorism seems to be gaining strength every day, as we can see from the recent downing of the Russian plane in the Sinai and the attacks in Paris. Clearly, we must be doing something wrong.

It should be obvious to anyone who thinks about terrorism and the global War on Terror that we have utterly failed to understand and address the root causes of terrorism. This is true whether we are talking about false-flag terrorism, such as 9/11, or real terrorism, such as what we see when Palestinians take up arms against the Israeli occupation. In the latter case, our leaders and the so-called "international community" have completely failed to address the grievous injustices suffered by the Palestinians living under Israeli occupation since 1948.

The day after the attacks in Paris on November 13, 2015, Margot Wallstrom, the Swedish foreign minister, appeared on Swedish TV and explained how the Israeli occupation was at the root of Palestinian violence, saying, "You come back to situations like that in the Middle East where not least the Palestinians see that there isn't any future (for them). (The Palestinians) either have to accept a desperate situation or resort to violence."

Unfortunately, there are few politicians in the Western world who are willing to articulate such common sense views, and even fewer who are willing to do something about it. Because the global community has failed to put pressure on Israel, the Zionist occupation has grown and intensified creating an extremely unjust situation that produces violence, as it will until an equitable solution is found.

As for false-flag terrorism, such as 9/11 and other atrocities, there is an appalling lack of moral courage on the part of world leaders to stand up and say that we have been deceived about what happened on 9/11. The failure on the part of our political, religious, and academic leaders to challenge the false narrative of 9/11 has enabled the fraudulent War on Terror to go on, at great expense to our nations and societies.

Rather than demanding an investigation of 9/11 and working from what the evidence proves, our leaders have allowed themselves to be deceived into war based on false media reports and lies from government officials. The fact that the 'crime of the century' was not even investigated as a crime does not seem to disturb the political and media elites of the United States. A false narrative was prepared ahead of time, as were military assets, and the war in Afghanistan began before the fires had been put out at the World Trade Center. The French military response after the attacks in Paris was even hastier, coming only two days later.

Today, fourteen years after 9/11, the terrorism that we are experiencing is beginning to look very much like that depicted in the Israeli-produced film, *Brazil*. This film, produced in 1985 by Arnon Milchan, Israel's nuclear-smuggling agent in Hollywood, is set in a bleak society in the future where senseless acts of terrorism occur frequently as the government wages war against terrorists in some distant land. Why did Milchan make this movie? Where did he get these ideas from?

We need to understand that Arnon Milchan is not just another Mossad agent in Hollywood; he is at the very top of the Israeli state intelligence/criminal network. In the Israeli-written biography, *Confidential: The Life Of Secret Agent Turned Hollywood Tycoon* (2011), it is revealed how Milchan was involved in espionage, big-ticket arms-dealing, and obtaining sensitive technology and materials for Israel's nuclear weapons program.

Interviewed regarding Milchan's intelligence activities, Israeli President Shimon Peres stated:

> Arnon is a special man. It was I who recruited him… When I was at the Ministry of Defense, Arnon was involved in numerous defense-related procurement activities and intelligence operations. His strength is in making connections at

the highest levels… His activities gave
us a huge advantage, strategically, diplo-
matically and technologically.

The authors established that "at least through the mid-1980s [Milchan] was a full-fledged operative for Israel's top-secret intelligence agency, LAKAM. His activities included "buying components to build and maintain Israel's nuclear arsenal" and supervising "government-backed accounts and front companies that financed the special needs of the entirety of Israel's intelligence operations outside the country."

Milchan clearly occupies a position at the very top of Israeli intelligence. Although he was at the center of an operation that smuggled hundreds of triggers for nuclear bombs to Israel, he was never prosecuted, while the people beneath him were. It is important to note that Benjamin Netanyahu worked for Milchan's company when this smuggling of nuclear triggers was being set up and carried out.

The terrorism in Milchan's film *Brazil* made in the 1980s shows an uncanny prescience of our world today. Milchan showed similar prescience of the events of 9/11 in his first film, *The Medusa Touch* (1978), in which a Boeing 747 crashes into the Pan Am Building in New York.

Later, in 2000, in the pilot episode of "The Lone Gunmen," a remotely-hijacked aircraft is flown into the World Trade Center. This television series was produced by Arnon Milchan's close friend and business partner, Rupert Murdoch.

Arnon Milchan, the Mossad Mogul of Hollywood, didn't dream up these terror scenarios on his own. These plots are clearly based on what Milchan knew about the plans of Israeli intelligence. He is, after all, a very close personal friend of Shimon Peres, the godfather and mastermind of Israel's high-tech military and unlawful nuclear arsenal.

More to the point, Shimon Peres has always supported the use of terror to coerce the West to support Israel's strategic goals. As Israel's prime minister Moshe Sharett wrote about Shimon Peres in 1955: "He wants to frighten the West into supporting Israel's aims."

As I explain in my *Solving 9/11* books, the false-flag terrorism of 9/11 was an Israeli idea from the beginning, first articulated by a former head of the Mossad in the 1970s. At the same time that Isser Harel was predicting how Arab terrorists would attack the tallest towers in New York City, Benjamin Netanyahu was holding an international conference of Western leaders in Jerusalem

(1979) to promote a global war against terrorism. Both concepts are products of Israeli strategic planners.

Today, Benjamin Netanyahu is the prime minister of Israel and his fraudulent War on Terror is in full swing. Western nations, including France, who seek to overthrow the elected government of Syria, are lining up to bomb a besieged nation that is virtually defenseless. The French military has now reacted to an unsolved act of terrorism by bombing Syria, as the United States bombed Afghanistan in October 2001 – without presenting any evidence to prove that the true source of the Paris attacks is from Syria.

The day after the attacks in Paris, French President François Hollande said, "An act of war was committed by a terrorist army, Daesh [ISIS], a jihadist army, against France... An act of war prepared, planned, from outside, with outside complicity which an investigation will establish."

This is almost identical to statements from U.S. leaders after 9/11 who took the nation to war saying that evidence to support their case would be presented in the near future. In the fourteen years since the invasion of Afghanistan, however, we have not seen one piece of evidence linking the Taliban with the events of

9/11. Our government and media were willing partners in the criminal deception that took the U.S. military into Afghanistan.

From the little we know about the terrorists in Paris, there is certainly not enough evidence to warrant a massive bombing campaign in Syria. For all we know the terrorists could have been controlled by a non-Syrian agency who wants France to bomb Syria. Now that the French police have killed Abdel Hamid Abaaoud, the Moroccan-Belgian who is said to be the mastermind of the attacks, there will be less information available to find the true source of the terrorism.

We can't accept that our leaders take our nations to war based merely on deceptions and illusions. We will never end terrorism by lashing out at the terrorist boogeyman and destroying nations in the process. The only way to end the fraudulent War on Terror is by exposing who is really behind terrorism and ending the deception.

If there was no American prison in Iraq, there would be no IS (Islamic State, ISIS, Daesh) now. Bucca was a factory. It made us all. It built our ideology.

Abu Ahmed, senior official of ISIS, "Isis: The Inside Story," *Guardian*, December 11, 2014

Chapter VIII

Creating the Foe

In reality, the War on Terror is an Israeli propaganda construct designed to deceive the West into destroying Israel's enemies on behalf of the Zionist state. The concept is essentially an Israeli war strategy, first promoted on the world stage by Benjamin Netanyahu and Menachem Begin (former terrorist founder of the Likud party) at the Jerusalem Conference hosted by the Netanyahu Institute in July 1979.

Former C.I.A. director George H.W. Bush spoke at the final session of the Jerusalem conference in support of waging war on terrorists. At the time, George Bush was running for president in the United States.

According to the War on Terror doctrine advocated by Netanyahu, "Islamic terrorists" attack Israel because it is a Western state with Western values. The West, Netanyahu says, is the real target so the U.S. must lead the West in waging a global war to destroy Islamic terrorists and the regimes that support them. This is exactly the ill-advised campaign the United States has engaged in since 9/11, at incredible expense to its own population and leaving a trail of devastated nations in its wake.

The Israeli construct was designed primarily to get the U.S. to destroy the enemies of the Zionist state. The Israelis developed the War on Terror construct and then created the Islamic opponent, Al Qaeda, to serve as the antithesis – the virulent enemy of the West. The real purpose of Al Qaeda, and its subsequent incarnations like ISIS, is to be a moving target that can be used to destabilize and destroy sovereign countries, like Syria, while sustaining the illusion of an Islamic foe, posing a mortal threat to the security of the West. The Zionist-controlled media is the essential element in selling the fraudulent war to the public.

The Soviet invasion of Afghanistan in 1979 gave Israel's military intelligence (AMAN) the perfect opportunity to create a cadre of anti-Western Islamic "terrorists", which would become the "enemy" in their fabricated War on Terror. From the early 1980s, the C.I.A. began a covert effort to support Afghan mujahideen in their 'holy struggle' or jihad, to remove the Red Army from Afghanistan. The allies who worked with the C.I.A. to arm the mujahideen were Israel, Saudi Arabia, and Pakistan.

An extremely pro-Israel Congressman from Texas, Charlie Wilson, acted as an Israeli weapons dealer in brokering an arrangement with Pakistani leader Mohammed Zia ul-Haq and Gulbuddin Hekmatyar to provide Israeli weapons (captured from the P.L.O. in Lebanon) and Israeli trainers for the Hezb-i-Islami mujahideen in Pakistan.

Wilson's Israeli handler was Zvi Rafiah, Mossad station chief in Washington, who had known Wilson since 1973 and who used his congressional office as if it were his own. As George Crile described in his book, *Charlie Wilson's War*, "Rafiah had always acted as if he owned Wilson's office. One of the staffers kept a list of people he needed to lobby. He would use the phones, give projects to the staff, and call on Charlie to intervene whenever he needed him."

Charlie Wilson got the notoriously anti-Western Gulbuddin Hekmatyar to accept weapons and training from the Israelis. But, why would the C.I.A. and the Israelis choose to arm the most radical and virulently anti-Western group of mujahideen, Hekmatyar's Hezb-i-Islami? Why would they not choose to arm a pro-Western Afghan militia that was more successful in combat, like that headed by the Pashtun leader Abdul Haq?

The lion's share of weaponry went to the anti-Western Hezb-i-Islami run by Gulbuddin Hekmatyar, Peter Bergen explains in *Holy War, Inc.: Inside the Secret World of Osama bin Laden.* "By the most conservative estimates, $600 million" in American aid went to Hekmatyar's party, which "had the dubious distinction of never winning a significant battle during the war, training a variety of militant Islamists from around the world, killing significant numbers of mujahideen from other parties, and taking a virulently anti-Western line."

While Israeli military intelligence agents posing as Arabs trained his group, by 1984 Gulbuddin had developed close ties with bin Laden, while receiving assistance from the C.I.A. and Pakistan's intelligence agency, the I.S.I.

Israeli military intelligence provided Hezb-i-Islami with weapons and trained at least 4,000 men in the anti-Western militia. Thousands of non-Afghan fighters joined Hezb-i-Islami, including thousands of Arabs, known as Afghan Arabs. Osama bin Laden is the most famous of the Afghan Arabs. Having trained a cadre of 4,000 anti-Western Islamic fighters, Israeli military intelligence and C.I.A. had a database of names to populate the Islamic anti-Western antithesis needed for the War on Terror construct. This database was known as Al Qaeda.

Having lost Saudi support when it supported Saddam Hussein, and Pakistani support after 1994, "the remainder of Hezb-i-Islami merged into al-Qaeda and the Taliban," according to the *Columbia World Dictionary of Islamism*.

A Hebrew-speaking double-agent of Egyptian origin, Ali Mohamed, was involved in the training of the Afghan Arabs. Mohamed trained Osama bin Laden, Ayman al-Zawahiri, and the terrorists responsible for the bombings of the two U.S. embassies in Africa. Mohamed is said to have been bin Laden's "first trainer". But, where and how did Mohamed learn Hebrew? And how did this Hebrew-speaking agent, involved in all the major Al Qaeda terror attacks of the 1990s and sentenced to life in prison, disappear without a trace from the U.S. judicial system?

The Hebrew-speaking Ali Mohamed runs like a red thread connecting all Al Qaeda terrorist activities during the 1990s as we learn from *United States of America* v. *Ali Mohamed*:

> In 1992, I conducted military and basic explosives training for Al Qaeda in Afghanistan... I also conducted intelligence training for Al Qaeda. I taught my trainees how to create cell structures that could be used for operations.

Ali Mohamed seems to have been the mastermind behind the terrorist attacks attributed to Al Qaeda. For example, while bin Laden and Ali Mohamed had reportedly discussed creating cells in Tanzania and Kenya, it was Ali Mohamed who went to Nairobi and actually set up the terrorist cell that carried out the bombings of the embassies.

Ehud Barak was head of Israel's Military Intelligence Directorate (AMAN 1983-1985) when Israeli military intelligence agents began arming and training Gulbuddin Hekmatyar's Hezb-i-Islami. If the Hebrew-speaking Ali Mohamed was training Osama bin Laden when the Israelis were in charge of training the Hezb-i-Islami terrorists, it seems most likely that Mohamed was working for Israeli military intelligence under its director, Ehud Barak.

But how do we form our opinions of the present? The West depends in large measure on its media. This is why terrorists, in their war against the West, devote so much of their strategy and their effort to capturing the Western press and using it for their own purposes.

Benjamin Netanyahu, *Terrorism: How the West Can Win* (1986)

Chapter IX

Who Makes the Terrorist Videos?

The historical record clearly shows that Israeli military intelligence developed and planned the doctrine of the War on Terror as a war strategy in the 1970s. Under the leadership of Ehud Barak, Israeli military intelligence then went on to create the cadre of Afghan-Arab terrorists in Pakistan in the 1980s, members of which became the nucleus of the Al Qaeda organization. Creating an Islamic foe for the War on Terror was a necessary element of the game.

The terrorism of 9/11 was designed to kick-start the long-planned War on Terror. Minutes after the planes struck the Twin Towers, Ehud Barak, the Israeli whose military intelligence agents had created, armed, and trained the bin Laden organization (in Pakistan) appeared on the BBC World television network blaming Osama bin Laden and calling for the U.S. to begin an "operational, concrete, war against terror."

Realizing that every aspect of the fraudulent War on Terror is controlled by Israeli military intelligence is essential to understanding the true nature of the wars being waged across the Middle East by the United States and its allies.

Propaganda is essential to steer the war and control how the public thinks about it. Here again we find Israeli intelligence controlling the release of propaganda videos supposedly created by the Islamic terrorists. In most cases the Western media and intelligence agencies are provided with the terrorist video and an interpretation of the video from an Israeli intelligence agent named Rita Katz, an Iraqi-born Israeli based in Bethesda, Maryland.

Through Katz, Israeli intelligence provides the propaganda and crafts the narrative about ISIS and the Middle East for the gullible U.S. media and politicians. By being the only source of the videos, Israeli intelligence is able to construct the terrorist narrative as it likes.

Katz founded the Search for International Terrorist Entities (SITE) Intelligence Group, a private intelligence firm, in July 2002. Western media outlets subscribe to her propaganda service and report on the videos giving source credit to SITE Intelligence Group, which is usually described as "U.S.-based" although there is nothing American about it. It is purely an Israeli intelligence operation set up to feed propaganda to the media and intelligence agencies in order to steer Israel's fraudulent War on Terror.

In many cases, Katz has released videos before they have been posted by the terrorist group that supposedly made them. What is odd about this is that the videos are coming to the media directly from Katz. By being the first and only source of the videos, Katz is able to control the timing of the release of the video and the interpretation of its content which are important aspects of propaganda.

Katz admitted on CNN that she had released a beheading video before ISIS had, explaining that her group had the video "beforehand." Now ask yourself, how could an Israeli intelligence agent in Maryland have a copy of the video before the terrorists who supposedly made the video had released it?

Katz has a long history of spreading videos before they have been posted by the terrorists. In 2007, for example, she released videos of Al Qaeda figures. On July 4, 2007, SITE distributed a video of Ayman al-Zawahiri ahead of its release by Al Qaeda's As-Sahab Media. U.S. and British intelligence officials were reportedly of the opinion that As-Sahab Media was run by Adam Gadahn (born Adam Pearlman), an American Jew who supposedly joined Al Qaeda in Pakistan in 1998.

Then, on September 7, 2007, SITE provided the Associated Press with what was supposedly a 30-minute video of Osama bin Laden, in which bin Laden's image is "frozen" for all but three minutes of the tape, a full day before Al Qaeda posted the video.

Rita Katz and SITE Intelligence Group have been providing propaganda videos since the War on Terror began. To this day her sources remain connected to Israeli intelligence.

WHO IS AL FURAT MEDIA?

Let's look at the grisly ISIS video from "Al Furat Media" supposedly showing the killing of a Russian soldier in May 2017 and examine how it came to Western media outlets. First, as usual, Rita Katz issued a Twitter message with photos and a link to the video from Al Furat Media. But what is Al Furat Media?

First, it seems strange that "Al Furat Media Foundation," who is evidently capable of producing high quality videos, does not even have a website. Why wouldn't this media outlet send its nasty and shocking videos directly to its chosen audience, in this case the Russian government or Russian media?

An online search for "Al Furat" finds four media outlets named Furat, but none of them are "Al Furat Media

Foundation." A search for Al Furat Media videos finds dozens of videos that supposedly come from ISIS and Furat Media, yet none of them actually come from a website belonging to an organization called "Al Furat." Rather, the videos all come from a website called Jihadology.net.

What is Jihadology.net? On its website it calls itself "a clearinghouse for jihadi primary source material." But, who runs this "clearinghouse for jihadi primary source material"?

Well, Jihadology.net is actually run by Aaron Yosef Zelin from Highland Park, Illinois. Zelin graduated from Brandeis University and works with Zionist think-tanks like the Washington Institute for Near East Policy.

Aaron Zelin speaks and writes about ISIS. His father, Richard D. Zelin, is a high-level Zionist in Chicago, and was Associate Director of the Jewish Community Relations Council of the Jewish United Fund and Director of the Chicago Conference on Soviet Jewry, among other things. How did this Zionist kid from Chicago become such an expert on ISIS?

Well, Aaron Zelin attends Israeli intelligence events like the International Institute for Counter-Terrorism's (ICT) 16th International Conference at Mossad's university, the Inter-Disciplinary Center (IDC) in Herzliya, the suburb of Tel Aviv where Mossad is based. This event opened on the evening of September 11, 2016. One of the key speakers was the Israeli-American dual-national Michael Chertoff, the former Asst. Attorney General who oversaw the destruction of the crucial evidence from the 9/11 bombings. The *Jewish Voice* reported that Aaron Zelin was one of the speakers at the five-day conference.

So, the "primary source material" of the "Al Furat" videos on the Internet is actually coming from an American Zionist who works very closely with Israeli military intelligence. This raises the logical question: Who is actually making these grisly videos and why are they all coming to us through Israeli agents like Rita Katz and Aaron Zelin? Shouldn't we be wary of accepting war propaganda material coming from the nation that dreamed up the War on Terror doctrine in the first place?

Are these videos actually being made by Israeli intelligence to frighten the West into supporting Israel's war agenda in the Middle East? That appears to be a very likely possibility that must be taken into consideration.

The best way to help Israel deal with Iran's growing nuclear capability is to help the people of Syria overthrow the regime of Bashar Assad.

Secretary of State Hillary Clinton in leaked email, December 31, 2012

The U.S. government insists it has the intelligence to prove it, but the American public has yet to see a single piece of concrete evidence – no satellite imagery, no transcripts of Syrian military communications – connecting the government of President Bashar Assad to the alleged chemical weapons attack last month that killed hundreds of people.

"Lingering doubts over Syria gas attack evidence"
Zeina Karam and Kimberly Dozier, AP, September 8, 2013

Chapter X

9/11 and the War in Syria

September 11, 2013

This year, the twelfth anniversary of 9/11, the com-
memoration of the victims is bound to be overshadowed
by the on-going political debate concerning President
Obama's threat to wage war against Syria. The U.S. Sen-
ate had actually scheduled a procedural vote for September 11 regarding Obama's proposed use of force. It may
very well be that the timing is no coincidence as these
two things, 9/11 and the war in Syria, are two parts of the
same strategic plan.

WAR OF TERROR

As 9/11 was the seminal event of the Israeli War on Terror,
the alleged use of chemical weapons by the Assad regime
of Syria is but the latest installment in this Zionist made-
for-television serial. Both events are examples of false-flag
terrorism in which the atrocity is blamed on the targeted
foe without presenting evidence to prove the case.

The Obama administration says it has evidence that Assad is responsible for the chemical attacks but refuses to present the evidence to the public. This is very odd because Obama wants public opinion to support his proposed use of force. How much sense does it make to claim you have evidence that you don't show?

It only makes sense if you understand how the War on Terror game is actually played. In this game of conquest, terrorism is the tactic, the method that is used to instigate and wage wars. The nations that are targeted have done nothing to deserve being invaded. They are attacked by terrorist gangs because the Zionist war planners have decided to wage war against them for some strategic interest, like the implementation of Israel's "Yinon Plan" which calls for the breaking up of the Arab states.

TERROR AS THEATER

In the War on Terror game the use of false-flag terrorism is a kind of theater which is played out to shock people and affect public opinion. Its primary purpose is to sway public opinion to support military action against the targeted foe who is quickly blamed for the atrocity. Because false-flag terror is theater there is no solid evidence to prove that the blamed foe really committed the atrocity, because he didn't actually carry out the deed. There can only be fabricated evidence because there is no real evidence to be presented. Most importantly, there is no real investigation and any attempt to investigate the crime is quickly shut down before it is able to expose the fraud.

Because the terrorist target is movable and changeable the War on Terror game can go on for decades. In the twelve years since 9/11, for example, we have seen the target moved from Afghanistan to Iraq, to Pakistan, to Yemen, to Libya, and now, to Syria and Iran, and these are just some of the targets.

Propaganda is an essential tool that is used to blame the targeted foe for the un-investigated atrocity. Since this involves lying to the public to take the nation to war, the people and politicians who push the lie are complicit in treason because they are working with and supporting the terrorists who actually carried out the atrocity.

In this way, George W. Bush, Dick Cheney, and Michael Chertoff (to name but a few) are complicit in the crimes of 9/11 including treason because they promoted the false story while preventing and obstructing a proper criminal investigation. Based on the lies about 9/11 Bush initiated two wars of aggression. These are among the most serious crimes a president can commit. There is ample evidence to bring George W. Bush to trial for treason and it is something that needs to happen.

Barack Obama is also complicit because he has failed to commission a proper investigation of 9/11. Rather than considering the evidence that the World Trade Center was demolished with sophisticated explosives, the Obama administration increased the war effort in Afghanistan and the use of drones to commit targeted killings in Afghanistan, Pakistan, and Yemen.

In May 2009 in Los Angeles, when Vice President Joe Biden was presented with a scientific paper proving that a form of super-thermite had been used to demolish the Twin Towers, he immediately turned on his heel and left the event – with the paper in hand.

Barack Obama and the officials in his administration cannot say they do not have the evidence that explosives were used to destroy the Twin Towers; they know that super-thermite and other explosives were used to kill nearly three thousand Americans on 9/11. That's the evil game they are playing; they cover-up the mass murder of 9/11 as they prepare to wage their next war of aggression.

To move ahead in the War on Terror game, the Obama administration now wants to attack Syria, claiming they have secret evidence that Assad gassed his own people. Once again, we are asked to believe these serious allegations without seeing any evidence. If Obama were to attack Syria it would be the third major war since 9/11 started in this deceitful way.

The good thing is that the American people and many world powers are strongly opposed to Obama's proposed use of force against Syria. The only people who actually support Obama's plan to aggress Syria are the Israelis and their Zionist agents in Congress, led by Senators John McCain and Lindsey Graham. That is to be expected, of course, because the War on Terror is an Israeli game developed and promoted by the Israeli prime minister Benjamin Netanyahu and his military intelligence apparatus.

The bad thing, however, is that the terrorism is not over yet. The War on Terror game will not be over until the people behind it are exposed, removed from office, and prosecuted for the crimes they have committed. This is why a complete and proper criminal investigation of 9/11 has to be done.

It is certainly not unreasonable to expect that such a criminal atrocity be fully investigated and prosecuted. A proper criminal investigation did not happen during the Bush administration because the person at the Department of Justice who was originally responsible for the 9/11 investigation and prosecution, the Israeli Michael Chertoff, was a key player in the conspiracy. He should be one of the first people arrested and charged for his role in the destruction of crucial evidence from the crimes of 9/11.

Twelve years later, we are still demanding – and still need – a complete criminal investigation into the events of 9/11. This is essential because until that happens we will not be able to free ourselves or our nation from the evil deception that has brought us two wars and taken the world to the brink of disaster.

Under U.S. law it is illegal for any American to provide money or assistance to Al Qaeda, ISIS or other terrorist groups. If you or I gave money, weapons, or support to Al Qaeda or ISIS, we would be thrown in jail. Yet the U.S. government has been violating this law for years, quietly supporting allies and partners of Al Qaeda, ISIL, Jabhat Fateh al Sham, and other terrorist groups with money, weapons, and intelligence support, in their fight to overthrow the Syrian government.

Rep. Tulsi Gabbard (D-Hawaii) introducing the Stop Arming Terrorists Act, December 8, 2016

Chapter XI

A Blank Check for Perpetual War

Three days after 9/11, after only two hours of debate, the U.S. Congress passed the Authorization for Use of Military Force (AUMF), a joint resolution giving the President the authority "to use all necessary and appropriate force against those nations, organizations, or persons he determines planned, authorized, committed, or aided the terrorist attacks that occurred on September 11, 2001." Signed into law by President George W. Bush on September 18, 2001, the AUMF is the Congressional authorization that funds the War on Terror operations.

Congresswoman Barbara Lee (D-Calif.) was the only member of Congress to vote against the resolution. In her statement of September 14, 2001, Lee said:

> We are not dealing with a conventional war. We cannot respond in a conventional manner. I do not want to see this

spiral out of control... we must be careful not to embark on an open-ended war with neither an exit strategy nor a focused target. We cannot repeat past mistakes.

A BLANK CHECK FOR PERPETUAL WAR

Rep. Lee's warning about the AUMF spiraling "out of control" and leading to "an open-ended war" has proved prophetic. In the first sixteen years of the War on Terror the AUMF resolution has been used for more than 37 military operations in 14 countries. Operation Inherent Resolve, for example, the current U.S. military operation in Iraq and Syria against the militant group known as the Islamic State of Iraq and the Levant (ISIL) is one of the 37 operations, although ISIL did not even exist in 2001. In September 2014, citing the AUMF, President Obama claimed that he had the authority he needed to wage war against ISIL.

After years of persistent effort, on June 29, 2017, Rep. Lee succeeded in getting her amendment approved by the House Appropriations Committee. If the final funding bill had gone through with Lee's amendment it would have given Congress 240 days to debate new authorization. At the end of the debate period, the 2001 AUMF would have been repealed.

"I've been working on this for years and years and years. I'm just really pleased that Republicans and Democrats today really understood what I've been saying and I've been explaining for the last 16 years, and that is, this resolution is a blank check for perpetual war," Lee said after her amendment passed the committee.

Before the vote, the congressmen who spoke in support of Lee's amendment said it was high time that Congress debate the authorization for the War on Terror. Several of them stressed that Congress had failed the members of the U.S. military by not debating the wars and operations to which they had been sent.

"Any administration can rely on this blank check to wage endless war," Lee told the committee members before the vote. "Many of us can also agree that a robust debate and vote is necessary, long overdue, and must take place."

Rep. Barbara Lee's hopes for a robust debate were dashed in the middle of the night on July 18 when House Republicans stripped her amendment from the Defense Department spending bill. House Speaker Paul D. Ryan (R-Wis.) was reported to be uncomfortable with the amendment.

One the same day Lee's amendment was approved, Ryan said: "There's a right way to deal with this, and an appropriations bill I don't think is the right way to deal with this. What matters to me is that we don't undercut the military, and whatever we do, we don't put ourselves, meaning the military, in a disadvantageous position."

The version of the bill that was approved by the House Rules Committee in the middle of the night replaced Lee's amendment with an amendment from Rep. Tom Cole (R-Okla.) that gives the White House 30 days to tell Congress its strategy for defeating Al Qaeda and Islamic State, and how the administration believes the current Authorization for the Use of Military Force applies.

Rep. Lee blamed Ryan for the removal of her amendment, saying: "Over the years, I've seen Republican leadership deploy every manner of undemocratic, underhanded tactics in Congress. But stripping my bipartisan amendment to repeal the 2001 AUMF – in the dead of night, without a vote – may be a new low from Speaker Ryan."

"Congress has been missing in action on matters of war and peace for nearly sixteen years. Republican leadership showed last night that they will do anything to maintain this status quo," Lee said. "Refusing to debate and vote on our ongoing wars is an abdication of our constitutional responsibility. Our men and women in uniform deserve better."

THIS MADNESS MUST END

Rep. Tulsi Gabbard (D-Hawaii) is another courageous congresswoman who has taken a stand against the duplicity of the War on Terror. In December 2016, Rep. Gabbard, an Iraq war veteran, introduced legislation which would prohibit the U.S. government from using American taxpayer dollars to provide funding, weapons, training, and intelligence support to groups like the Levant Front, Fursan al Haqq, and other allies of Jabhat Fateh al-Sham, Al Qaeda, and ISIS, or to countries who are providing direct or indirect support to those same groups.

In introducing the Stop Arming Terrorists Act on December 8, 2016, Gabbard said the U.S. government has been "quietly supporting allies and partners of Al Qaeda, ISIL, Jabhat Fateh al Sham and other terrorist groups with money, weapons, and intelligence support, in their fight to overthrow the Syrian government. The CIA has also been funneling weapons and money through Saudi Arabia, Turkey, Qatar and others who provide direct and indirect support to groups like ISIS and Al Qaeda. This support has allowed Al Qaeda and their fellow terrorist organizations to establish strongholds throughout Syria, including in Aleppo."

"This madness must end. We must stop arming terrorists," Gabbard concluded. "The Government must end this hypocrisy and abide by the same laws that apply to its citizens."

The legislation proposed by these two brave congresswomen indicates there is an urgent need for a real congressional debate on the AUMF and the military operations being waged under the pretext of fighting terrorism. After nearly sixteen years of senseless war in Afghanistan, the fighting and dying continues and the cost of the war increases by $4 million per hour, or nearly $100 million per day, according to the National Priorities Project. The war in Afghanistan has already cost more than $778 billion (as of July 2017) and the total cost of the wars fought since 9/11 exceeds $1.7 trillion. One might ask, if it weren't for Rep. Lee prodding them at what point would Congress take action to rein in the runaway War on Terror?

Rep. Gabbard's Stop Arming Terrorists Act should broaden the debate and open the discussion about the duplicity of the U.S. intervention in Syria. Gabbard's bill indicates that a covert strategy is at work that the public is generally not aware of. The U.S. has provided "direct and indirect support to groups like ISIS and Al Qaeda," Gabbard said when she introduced the bill. These are the very same groups the U.S. is supposedly fighting in the War on Terror. Why would the U.S. be supporting the avowed enemy of Operation Inherent Resolve in Syria? Shouldn't this be a subject of discussion and investigation by the media? Why isn't it?

For a person with a conventional understanding of the War on Terror, informed by the mainstream media, it certainly makes no sense that the U.S. would be supporting groups like ISIS and Al Qaeda, against which it is supposedly waging war. It isn't that Rep. Gabbard is misinformed, rather it is the public that has been misinformed and deceived for years about the true purpose of the War on Terror operations, like the anti-ISIS operation in Syria and Iraq.

The fact that the U.S. and its allies have supported terrorist groups like ISIS and Al Qaeda indicates that these groups are being used to advance the real strategy of the U.S.-led operation in Syria. The U.S. intervention in Syria began in 2013 under President Barack Obama and Secretary of State Hillary Clinton. In an email written by Secretary Clinton in December 2012, leaked by Wikileaks, she reveals that the U.S. policy to overthrow the Syrian government was being pursued to help Israel. Clinton's email said: "The best way to help Israel deal with Iran's growing nuclear capability is to help the people of Syria overthrow the regime of Bashar Assad."

This is a very important revelation because it indicates that the real reason the U.S. has intervened in Syria is not to fight terror, but to overthrow the government because it would be "the best way to help Israel deal with Iran's growing nuclear capability." When we understand that the Israeli strategic plan (i.e. Yinon Plan) for Iraq and Syria calls for splintering these nations into ethnic or religious enclaves we can make sense of U.S. support for groups like ISIS and Al Qaeda. They are being used to break up these multi-ethnic secular Arab states in order to advance the Zionist plan to dominate the Middle East.

The idea that Syria should be broken up into ethnic enclaves is pushed by Israeli officials and by the Zionist-controlled media as the only solution to the conflict. Israeli Defense Minister Moshe Yaalon, for example, at the Munich Security Conference on February 14, 2016, said:

> Unfortunately we are going to face chronic instability for a very, very long period of time… And part of any grand strategy is to avoid the past, saying we are going to unify Syria. We know how to make an omelette from an egg. I don't know how to make an egg from an omelette… We should realize that we are going to see enclaves, Alawistan, Syrian

Kurdistan, Syrian Druzistan. They might cooperate or fight each other.

On the same day, Ram Ben-Barak, Director General of Israel's Intelligence Ministry, spoke on Israel's Army Radio saying, "I think that, ultimately, Syria should be turned into regions under the control of whoever is there – the Alawites where they are, the Sunnis where they are." A partition of the Syrian state along sectarian lines was "the only possible solution," Ben-Barak said.

In order to make sense of the reports of U.S. support for jihadist militants and terrorist groups in Syria it is essential to understand that the War on Terror is really just a misleading cover to deceive the public about the real operational plan at work, which is to break Syria into ethnic enclaves as called for in the Yinon Plan, "The Zionist Plan for the Middle East." With this understanding of the deceptive nature of the War on Terror we are better able to make sense of the confusing developments and reports coming from the Middle East.

The truth is, there is no Islamic army or terrorist group called Al Qaeda. And any informed intelligence officer knows this. But there is a propaganda campaign to make the public believe in the presence of an identified entity representing the 'devil' only in order to drive the 'TV watcher' to accept a unified international leadership for a war against terrorism.

Pierre-Henri Bunel, former French artillery and intelligence officer, "Al Qaeda: The Data Base" as cited in Wayne Madsen Report, November 20, 2005

Chapter XII

It's All Good: The Illusion

The War on Terror has destroyed the lives of millions, including thousands of Americans. It has grossly perverted our thinking and plundered our national wealth. Although it is the longest war in U.S. history there is virtually no public resistance or anti-war movement protesting against it. This book should help people grasp the essential deception of the War on Terror. We can only resist the war if we understand what it is.

The wars or "operations", as they are conveniently called, waged since 9/11 under the pretext of fighting terrorism are costing U.S. taxpayers $8.36 million per hour, for a total of $1.75 trillion since 2001. Homeland Security, the domestic front against terrorism, is costing U.S. taxpayers $6.74 million per hour, or nearly $750 billion since 9/11. Together, the foreign and the domestic security operations have cost the U.S. more than $2.5 trillion (i.e. 2,500 billions) according to the National Priorities Project (NPP).

The Costs of War Project of the Watson Institute at Brown University, which includes in its calculations "hidden or unacknowledged costs of the U.S. decision to respond to the 9/11 attacks with military force," puts the total costs of Homeland Security and the wars in Iraq, Afghanistan, Pakistan, and Syria, from 2001 through 2016 at $4.8 trillion, nearly twice the figure given by the NPP.

In any case such outrageous expenditures on the so-called War on Terror are clearly not sustainable. Rather than rebuilding America and taking care of the vital needs of the population, we are pouring billions of borrowed dollars down the drain in unnecessary wars. These foreign wars have failed to benefit the American people, or the world, in any way. We are squandering money to destroy lives, nations, and infrastructure across the Middle East like the worst of barbarians, and have been doing so at a ferocious rate for 26 years – continuously since Desert Storm in January 1991.

With all the wars, and millions of displaced refugees trekking about the planet, you might expect there would be a vibrant anti-war movement of concerned citizens demanding an end to the warfighting, but there isn't. Why are Americans not standing up in huge numbers and demanding an end to this utterly self-destructive War on Terror?

IT'S ALL GOOD

The answer is simple. We have been deceived, as individuals and a nation, into thinking that the War on Terror is a good thing, a valiant struggle against terrorists who intend to attack us like we were attacked on September 11, 2001. I will use a comment from a reader to a recent post of mine to illustrate my point.

I had posted something about the estimated 26,171 bombs dropped by the United States in 2016, under a president who had been awarded the Nobel Peace Prize when he was elected in 2008. Last year was the fifteenth year of the War on Terror, a year in which the U.S. bombed seven nations, dropping an average of 72 bombs per day.

Most of the bombs were dropped in Iraq and Syria: 12,192 in Syria and 12,095 in Iraq. Afghanistan was bombed 1,337 times and Libya 496. The numbers are based on the percentage of total coalition airstrikes carried out in 2016 by the United States in Operation Inherent Resolve (OIR), the counter-Islamic State campaign.

In response, I had the following exchange with a reader in Idaho:

> **D.S.:** Well, if it's killing people who are killing innocent people, it's all good.

Bollyn: This is a very good comment because it reflects the thought that the masterminds behind the War on Terror want us to think. That our warfighting in the Middle East is all about killing the bad guys in order to bring about good. It is, of course, not why we are fighting in Iraq or Syria. When was the last time the U.S. went to war to stop the killing of innocents?

When Israel invaded Lebanon in 1982 and killed 20,000 innocents, did the U.S. intervene to stop them? When Israel attacks Gaza and kills thousands of innocents, does the U.S. do anything to stop them?

No. So why would the U.S. do something in Syria or Iraq that it has never done? We are not waging war in Iraq or Syria to protect innocent lives – that is the propaganda cover story that has worked amazingly well to neutralize any anti-war movement from gaining traction, but I am still trying.

D.S.: And you think different? How about you go and give them a big wet sloppy kiss then. When was the last time we went to war to stop the killing of innocents? Well, when Saddam invaded Kuwait comes to mind, did you forget that?

Bollyn: We certainly did not go to war against Iraq to save the lives of innocent people – again, that was the propaganda we were given (e.g. the contrived testimony from the daughter of the Kuwaiti ambassador about the babies being killed). Apart from the thousands we killed in Desert Storm in 1991, we then put sanctions on Iraq that led to the deaths of hundreds of thousands of children. You may recall Leslie Stahl's interview with Secretary of State Madeline Albright about the U.S.-imposed sanctions having killed 500,000 Iraqi babies?

D.S.: So, in a nut shell, you say we are the villains, and should mind our own business, as all this is trouble in the Middle

East we brought on? I agree, we helped them out in WWII, and then we had the audacity to find oil there, and show them how to pump it out of the ground. Yep, it's all America's fault.

Bollyn: No, we are not the villains; we are the deceived. I do agree, however, that we should mind our own business and stay out of these foreign conflicts. 9/11 was a false-flag deception to start the War on Terror, which is an Israeli war agenda to dominate the region by destroying the large Arab states and breaking them into weak ethnic enclaves – at war with each other.

To understand how this foreign Zionist agenda was pushed onto our military in the wake of 9/11, there is a photo from January 2002 at the Pentagon showing the Israeli Chief of Staff, Shaul Mofaz, meeting with the Zionist Neo-Cons (Paul Wolfowitz, Dov Zakheim, and Douglas Feith) who made up the Defense Policy Board under President George Bush. The list had evidently already been drawn up of the seven Middle Eastern nations that the U.S. would overthrow in the next five years: Iraq,

Syria, Libya, Sudan, Somalia, Lebanon, and Iran. Five of which have already been done.

This is not a war being fought for U.S. interests, but a Zionist/Israeli war agenda disguised as the War on Terror. There is no real U.S. national interest in this criminal war of aggression – none. Our nation has been deceived, perverted, and plundered in order to wage these wars under the pretext of fighting terrorism.

Nothing on earth can ever justify a crime ...
If you grant an amnesty to the past, you are corrupting the future.

Benjamin Constant, *Des Effets de la Terreur* (1797)

Chapter XIII

How Will the War on Terror End?

The false-flag terror attacks of 9/11 and the War on Terror are two prongs of a dual deception. Now that this is exposed and understood one might ask, how can it go on?

I often wonder how the War on Terror will end. Knowing it is an artificially imposed "reality", I wonder if it will be allowed to just peter out and disappear quietly from the scene, or will it be maintained and increased? A fraud of this magnitude simply cannot be kept up forever. With the election of Donald Trump, this is a central question facing the new administration and the nation.

The War on Terror is, after all, a completely artificial war that has been imposed on us through deceit. Since 9/11, this deception has been maintained by phony acts of terrorism and contrived armies of Islamic extremists. Sixteen years after being given a global mandate by Congress to use force against the terrorists who attacked us, the U.S. is currently waging war in at least a half-dozen nations under the pretext of fighting terrorism.

The false-flag terror atrocity of 9/11 was meant to kick-start the War on Terror, a Zionist war agenda in disguise that had been pushed by Benjamin Netanyahu since the late 1970s. The crimes of 9/11 were not investigated because they were not meant to be scrutinized or solved. This means that the worst criminal atrocity in American history in which some 3,000 civilians were killed has never been properly investigated as a crime.

Since the 9/11 attacks were meant to initiate the War on Terror the public was given a fabricated narrative that Osama bin Laden and his gang of Islamist terrorists attacked the United States simply because they hate our freedom. Calling the 9/11 crime an act of war the Bush administration refused to investigate the crime, declared war on terrorism, destroyed the crucial evidence, and promptly invaded Afghanistan.

The Bush administration did not begin a criminal investigation of the terror attacks of 9/11 because an investigation would have exposed the narrative as fiction. A forensic investigation would have revealed that the crime had not been carried out by Muslims, but was a false-flag attack designed and executed by Israeli military intelligence in order to be blamed on Muslims and start their long-planned War on Terror.

Exposing the cover story as fictitious would have stopped the Israeli War on Terror in its tracks and turned the spotlight right on the Zionist masterminds of 9/11.

I have written two letters to Donald Trump in the past year asking if he would call for an investigation of 9/11 as president, but I have not received a response from the White House.

The terrorism of 9/11 and the War on Terror are two parts of a dual deception designed to trick the United States and its allies into fighting a Zionist war agenda in the Middle East. Enslaved to this deception, we have been waging war for Israel for the past sixteen years.

While the War on Terror is an obvious fraud and deception, the wars being fought in its name have very real costs. Tens of thousands of Americans have been killed or injured in these artificial wars, which have cost the U.S. trillions of borrowed dollars. Millions of innocent people have been killed, wounded, and displaced in the countries where these wars have been waged. How much longer can this evil deception go on? How can America survive when it is spending hundreds of millions of dollars a day on unnecessary and illegal wars of aggression?

We have been burdened with this lawless and fraudulent Zionist war agenda since 2001, imposed on us through the deception of 9/11. Regime change and Balkanization are the tactics of the criminal cabal behind this deception, tactics which have been employed on countries from Afghanistan to Libya, Iraq, and Ukraine. Syria is the latest victim of these criminal predators.

All of this is, of course, highly illegal, which is why I ask, how will this all end? How will the culprits manage the climb-down? A growing number of people are aware of the deception of 9/11 and the War on Terror, and who is behind it. The question being asked is: Will Donald Trump, a friend of Benjamin Netanyahu and other hardcore Zionists, bring the War on Terror to an end – or make it worse?

Similar political constellations of U.S. and Israeli leaders have led to extreme violence: Ronald Reagan and Menachem Begin led to the Israeli invasion of Lebanon in 1982, and George W. Bush and Ariel Sharon led to 9/11 and the War on Terror in 2001. Will Donald Trump and Benjamin Netanyahu bring us something better?

As a presidential candidate Donald Trump said he was opposed to the regime change policies of the Bush and Obama administrations, the modus operandi of the War on Terror:

"Hillary Clinton's support for violent regime change in Syria has thrown the country into one of the bloodiest civil wars anyone has ever seen – while giving ISIS a launching pad for terrorism against the West."
- Donald Trump, June 22, 2016

"Our current strategy of nation-building and regime change is a proven failure. We have created the vacuums that allow terrorists to grow and thrive."
- Donald Trump, August 15, 2016

Not only has this strategy been a failure – it has been a criminal enterprise, which means that people like Barack Obama, Hillary Clinton, and George Bush are culpable for some very serious crimes. Apart from being a failure, such criminal activity destroys American prestige and credibility around the world.

If Donald Trump is truly serious about "draining the swamp" in Washington, he should start with a criminal investigation of the Obama and Bush administrations. If Trump were to pardon Obama, as Obama pardoned Bush, he would be allowing the presidents who have committed treasonous crimes during the past 15 years to retire in luxury at taxpayer expense. This is highly destructive to our nation because such blanket pardons enable the criminal network to get away with mass murder and treason. More importantly, we are allowing our great republic to be turned into a rogue state headed by criminals.

L ook back through history and you will see that
big change comes from movements – not from
politicians.

Philip R. Warth, former President and CEO of Feeding
America

Chapter XIV

What Can We Do?

"What can we do?" is the question people ask most frequently after they have grasped the essence of the monstrous deception behind 9/11 and the War on Terror. Understanding that we have been deceived about the terror atrocity that changed the world and the wars that followed in its aftermath, concerned citizens naturally wonder what they can do to help rectify the situation.

Americans, like the citizens of other Western nations, tend to think that their democratic systems work. Most people believe that the state structure is equipped with adequate safeguards and institutions to prevent criminal atrocities like 9/11 from happening. When, however, such heinous crimes do occur, people trust that the government will thoroughly investigate the crime, find and prosecute the guilty, and that the media will inform the public of the evidence and important facts of the case.

The fact that the evidence and truth about the 9/11 atrocity have been covered up and ignored by the government and media shows that our faith in the system is misplaced – it does not work. If it were simply a matter of one corrupt or incompetent president then we would expect to see a change with a new administration in the White House. In the case of 9/11, however, we have had three presidents and not one of them has addressed the subject of 9/11 truth or even suggested an end to the disastrous wars being waged under the pretext of fighting terrorism. The 9/11 Wars, another term for the disastrous wars in Afghanistan and Iraq, are the longest wars in U.S. history yet there seems to be no political will to end them.

If the government and media will not address the deception of 9/11 and the War on Terror, the most important political issue of our time, how can we possibly expect them to rectify the situation? Since the government and media are involved in the criminal cover-up of 9/11 we have to conclude that they are controlled by the very same people who carried out the crime itself. The only people who benefit from the 9/11 cover-up are the masterminds who planned it. Likewise, the government and media have promoted the War on Terror, a criminal agenda to wage wars of aggression in order to overthrow national governments and redraw the map of the Middle East.

Facing such a massive criminal deception of global importance one would expect our universities and churches to embrace the pursuit of 9/11 truth, but there is virtually no support coming from these fundamental pillars of our democratic society. So effective and complete is the deception that there is no organized resistance to the unjust wars that began more than sixteen years ago.

This is why it is incumbent on the individual who comprehends the deception behind 9/11 and the War on Terror to spread awareness of the truth. The deception has no power of its own. The only power the lies have is that of the people who believe them. The deception is only as strong as those who are deceived and the only way to undeceive people is to inform them of the truth.

This is what we can do, and it is the most effective way to deal with such deception. Spread the truth by discussing the subject with your friends and family whenever appropriate. If they express interest in knowing more about 9/11 and the War on Terror, share this book and my *Solving 9/11* books with them. Every individual who is disabused of this awful deception will become a soldier of truth, and will be forever grateful to the person who helped them out of their deceived state by enlightening them and opening their eyes to the truth.

A person who comprehends the 9/11 deception will naturally want to share their understanding and awareness with others. For some it may be possible to join or organize a group where such political subjects are discussed. Public libraries usually offer meeting rooms for groups free of charge. Being part of a group empowers people as they share information with like-minded citizens. I have seen amazing 9/11 truth groups, like the one in San Diego, that organize monthly events and public outreach efforts through which they have shared 9/11 truth with thousands of people.

Although spreading the truth about 9/11 and the War on Terror may seem like a small thing in the face of such a massive deception, it is the most important thing we can do. We are doing a great service to our family and friends when we share the truth with them because a deceived person is likely to hold views and take actions that are detrimental to their own well-being and prosperity. A misinformed person, under the spell of the lies about 9/11 and the War on Terror, is unable to make the right choices and decisions because the information they are working with is false.

With increased understanding a person is prepared to stand up against the deception that has changed the world. Writing letters to our Congressmen and local newspapers is one way to spread this awareness. As more people become aware of the truth about 9/11 and the War on Terror the growing awareness will become a movement that will be able to bring about real change. We are the people who are building that movement by increasing awareness of the truth one person at a time.

Let no man deceive you by any means: for that day shall not come, except there come a falling away first, and that man of sin be revealed, the son of perdition.

2 Thessalonians 2:3, King James Bible

An American Muslim Perspective

9/11 & the 'Man of Sin'
The Nation of Islam Research Group
July 2017

The Honorable Elijah Muhammad is the man we in the Nation of Islam refer to as The Messenger of Allah. He is the great leader, teacher, and guide to some of the most powerful thinkers and leaders that Black people have ever produced. He once said to his finest student, The Honorable Minister Louis Farrakhan, "Brother, you cannot fathom the depths of Satan." This profound decree was meant to aid us in comprehending the long and diabolical history of terrorism committed against the Black man and woman in America and around the globe. With the execution of 9/11 in 2001, it is now apparent that The Messenger's words have reached far beyond the Black experience and apply most fittingly to a satanic global reality facing *all* of humanity.

Just days after 9/11, the Nation of Islam leadership was holding a conference a few miles outside Chicago.

The September 11 "attacks" were not on the agenda of that long-planned meeting but they were most assuredly on everyone's minds. Already, the official government story with its 19 box-cutter-wielding Arab skyjackers, and a cave-dwelling Islamic Svengali named Osama was thoroughly unbelieved.

How unusual that three skyscrapers collapsed so suddenly and completely into their own footprints. How strange that the government was able to pinpoint the perpetrator with a full biography within minutes. How convenient that 19 photos of the "terrorists" should become available in the media so quickly. And how miraculous was it that a passport of one of the "hijackers" should happen to fall 110 floors, unscathed, and land – not into the smoking ruins, but into the waiting hands of the police?

The most puzzling question was why? Why would any Muslim, even if he were inclined to violate every Quranic principle of human rights, choose that particular time when world politics was moving in favor of Palestinian rights (and against the repressive apartheid, militarist state of Israel) to needlessly ignite a War Against Islam? These were among the many questions being pondered in the Nation of Islam in the immediate aftermath of the 9/11 onslaught.

Just five days after 9/11, The Honorable Minister

Louis Farrakhan held a press conference and spoke for all of us:

> I, like millions of people around this earth, watched in amazement, shock, and horror, the events of September 11, and the unfolding of the ripple effect of this terrible tragedy.

Then he reminded a rushing-to-judgment America that,

> As a Muslim, it reads in the Qur'an as guidance for us: 'Whenever an unrighteous person brings you news, look carefully into it lest you harm a people in ignorance, then be sorry for what you did.' I remember President Johnson made the war in Vietnam the centerpiece of his administration and a great lie was told, [and] the Congress produced the Tonkin Gulf Resolution that led to 500,000 American soldiers being sent to Vietnam. It's unfortunate that one of the first casualties in war is the truth.

We were in the early stages of a newly declared "9/11

Nation," a new incarnation of America, with the U.S. Constitution violently supplanted by both an all-powerful 9/11 mythology in the form of government and media propaganda, and a draconian surveillance state in the form of the USA PATRIOT Act. The U.S. is now a False Flag Nation, so desperately corrupt that it marks its milestones by the atrocities it commits upon itself. But The Minister and the Nation of Islam – having been the constant target of false-flag, government-sponsored, Zionist/COINTELPRO terrorism – have resisted falling victim to this new satanic paradigm.

The Minister wrote to President George W. Bush in December 2001, decrying the "consistent pattern of behavior of America's Presidents, administrations, and the press" toward Muslim leaders and their using those leaders "as a justification for military action to cover their real purposes." Bush's only response was ramping up American military operations in the oil-rich Middle East, in what he called a "War on Terror."

On December 16, 2001, The Minister spoke in Phoenix and gave a clear picture of the aims or "real purposes" of America's leaders. Working from a map of the Middle East and Asia, he elucidated the plans for an oil pipeline to be routed through Taliban territory in Afghanistan and gave an overview of the political dynamics of that resource-rich region, in which he has traveled extensively.

The Messenger's warning about the "depths of Satan" was beginning to make much more sense.

Then came the revelation that just a year before 9/11 a group of pro-Israel Neoconservatives had formed the Project for a New American Century (PNAC) and called for "some catastrophic and catalyzing event, like a new Pearl Harbor," in their diabolical desire to reorder the Middle East. General Wesley Clark reinforced this with his uncovering of the Neocons' plan to take down "seven countries in five years." One by one the pillars of the official story – that of a cave-bound Osama leading an improvised box-cutter air force against an ill-defended and inept U.S. military machine – began to crumble and fall away. By degrees the "Man of Sin" of 2 Thessalonians 2:3 was being revealed.

Throughout, we watched the total capitulation of the corporate media, no longer a force for truth and objective analysis (not that they ever had been). Reporters, correspondents, and columnists abandoned journalism *en masse* and joined the ranks of the "crisis actors," a coordinated fraternity of deceivers tasked with diverting, confusing, and misleading the public. Fighting back and armed with an explosive media technology came a new community of Internet-based truth-seekers. They released often crude but always probing video investigations of a litany of 9/11 anomalies. Some of those amateur documentaries, such as *In Plane Site* and *Loose Change*, had far-reaching impact, and Nation of Islam members were some of the first to find and spread those critical tools to obliterate the mythologies that had fueled a global war policy.

As powerful and insightful as those productions were, they yet focused almost entirely on the absurdities and impossibilities of the official story. An organization emerged to professionalize the analysis of the 9/11 evidence. In 2006, architect Richard Gage was moved by the blatant anomalies of the World Trade Center tower collapses to form Architects & Engineers for 9/11 Truth. Hundreds of architects and engineers soon signed on, effectively moving the debate from the political to the scientific realm, and for the first time masters of the building sciences weighed in on the discussion in an organized way.

The Honorable Minister Louis Farrakhan has been the lone prominent voice in the religious world to consistently raise questions about 9/11. In 2012, he called for "a scientific analysis of 9/11" and brought to Chicago Mr. Gage and Kevin Ryan, a chemist whistle blower at the National Institute of Standards and Technology (NIST) who publicly questioned the World Trade Center investigation. They presented their findings at the annual Saviours' Day convention of the Nation of Islam and convincingly proved that America's "new Pearl Harbor" was not a product of Arabs or Muslims and that science itself was on the side of the 9/11 skeptics.

But that left one question that could not be asked: If not Arabs or Muslims, then *who* perpetrated the worst terrorist attack on American soil?

By now it was dawning on those who were pursuing the real perpetrators behind 9/11 that the evidence invariably pointed to the Middle East – but not to the "usual suspects." The fingerprints of Tel Aviv and the Israeli Mossad were all over the horrific events of 9/11. Though that truth was being circulated widely among the most ardent 9/11 truth-seekers, it was only discussed in whispers and hushed tones.

Journalist Christopher Bollyn was among the first to objectively cover the 9/11 atrocity. His reporting was distinguished for its unrelenting pursuit of the truth and his dogged determination to uncover the many layers and levels of this unfolding crime. His research confirmed that Israel and its Zionist operatives committed 9/11 as a false-flag operation – the largest and most elaborate of the many Israel has committed for its own wicked ends.

The reality of Israel's central role in 9/11 has shocked most, but the Nation of Islam has been steeled by its core teaching that Satan's absolute assignment is to deceive the whole world. The Most Honorable Elijah Muhammad made a harsh assessment in his 1965 book *Message to the Blackman*:

> That old serpent, called the devil and Satan, which deceiveth the whole world (Rev. 12:9) is a person or persons whose characteristics are like that of a serpent (snake). Serpents or snakes of the grafted type cannot be trusted, for they will strike you when you are not expecting a strike.

To many Christians (and Muslims), Jews have achieved a holy and sanctified level in the divine order of things as the Chosen People of God. That exalted position has blinded the world to some very Serpent-like behaviors – grievous historical and current actions – and shielded Jews from interrogation about some of the world's most egregious sins:

- The massive Jewish role in the trans-Atlantic slave trade was almost unknown until the 1990s.

- The rabbinical origin of the biblical "Curse of Ham," which assigns inferiority to black skin, has infected all religious traditions – even Islam.

- The sharecropping system that replaced and

continued chattel slavery in America was largely a Jewish enterprise.

- The central role of Jews in helping to construct the apartheid systems of South Africa has only recently come to light.

- The ongoing Israeli genocide against the Palestinians is now an open sore.

And so, for the Nation of Islam, 9/11 is merely the continuation of a satanic pattern of behavior by a people the world will soon come to know.

In February of 2017, Christopher Bollyn and his wife, Helje, graciously accepted the invitation of Minister Farrakhan to come to Detroit to address the Nation of Islam's annual Saviours' Day convention. The Bollyns joined two other American patriots, Islamic scholar Dr. Kevin Barrett and architect Richard Gage of Architects & Engineers for 9/11 Truth, who gave an encore presentation, for a program titled "The War on Islam: Israel & 9/11 Revisited, Uncovered and Exposed." Together they presented a forceful and conclusive case against Israel for the crime of the century and the many false-flag attacks that followed. Thousands attended that plenary session, which was said to be the largest audience to ever attend a 9/11 truth event.

Mr. Bollyn's latest book, *The War on Terror: The Plot to Rule the Middle East,* furthers the mighty mission of uncovering the truth of 9/11. He may not be aware of how significant his work is in the divine order. The satanic minds that now run the earth were incisively targeted and biblically contextualized by The Most Honorable Elijah Muhammad in 1974:

> Jesus came to the Jews and not to us and then he got disappointed that he was ahead of the time of the Jews to preach the doctrine of the destruction or judgment and the setting up of a New Kingdom of Heaven after the destruction of the Jew's civilization. Jesus was born two thousand years ahead of the judgment of the Jews.

Those who have come to the reality of 9/11 and contemplated the level of wickedness that produced it must understand that we are now in *that* time. Truth is the only weapon that the Righteous are given. But God promises that truth will be enough. The Holy Qur'an says: "We hurl the Truth against falsehood, so It knocks out its brains, and lo! it vanishes."

The next generation of humanity's struggle for truth seems destined for a final showdown. With the truth of 9/11 being revealed, a great separation – a "falling away," as 2 Thessalonians 2:3 prophesies – is occurring in the world before our very eyes. The Honorable Minister Louis Farrakhan's call for a boycott of the economic bloodlines that keep this serpent afloat is one that the 9/11 truth community – which now numbers in the millions – must also adopt.

In his very last speech in Memphis, Tennessee, in 1968, the Rev. Dr. Martin Luther King said that when we Blacks feel pain, we must "redistribute the pain." He specifically said the targeting of the economy through boycotts and strategic buying forces results from a people who understand nothing but Mammon (Luke 16:13). Dr. King called this strategy "Economic Withdrawal," and that is exactly where our truth activism is headed. The international Boycott, Divestment, and Sanction (BDS) movement has targeted the state of Israel economically for its brutal mistreatment of the Palestinians and as a consequence has done irreparable economic, political, and reputational harm to Israel's apartheid regime.

9/11 truth-tellers must also recognize the economic weaponry we have to bring the perpetrators to justice. The religious communities are becoming more aware that the so-called Jewish State may never have been worthy of the name. In July 2017, the 2.1 million-member Mennonite Church USA voted to boycott Israel. Days before that, the one million-member United Church of Christ overwhelmingly approved a resolution condemning Israel for its heinous treatment of the Palestinian people.

Going forward will require that the righteous from among *all* people of the earth unify – but unity around the truth is all that God will accept in this critical hour. There are no sidelines today; there can be no fence-sitters in this time; therefore, it is imperative that we fortify ourselves with intellectual armaments such as *The War on Terror: The Plot to Rule the Middle East,* and within our little spheres we must nudge our fellow citizens to embrace the manifest truth. In fact, we in the Nation of Islam hear in the appeal of Mr. Bollyn a very powerful truth that must be heeded:

> We have to re-claim our reality. We simply cannot let evil scoundrels impose an artificial reality and false history upon us. People who are deceived into war are not free people. A nation deceived is a nation enslaved. We cannot thrive as a nation if we are burdened with such an evil deception.

Selected Sources

"A Day of Terror: The Israelis; Spilled Blood Is Seen as Bond That Draws 2 Nations Closer," James Bennett, *New York Times*, September 12, 2001

Charlie Wilson's War by George Crile, Grove Press, 2003

Confidential: The Life of Secret Agent Turned Hollywood Tycoon – Arnon Milchan by Meir Doron and Joseph Gelman, Gefen Books, 2011

Cost of Military Programs, National Priorities Project (NPP), nationalpriorities.org, accessed June 27, 2017.

Costs of War Project, Watson Institute, Brown University, watson.brown.edu/costsofwar/, accessed June 27, 2017

Fighting Terrorism: How Democracies Can Defeat Domestic and International Terrorists, Benjamin Netanyahu, Farrar, Straus and Giroux, 1995

Hillary Clinton Email Archive, New Iran and Syria 2.Doc, Wikileaks.org, accessed July 5, 2017

"How Israel Created the Fiend for the War on Terror," Christopher Bollyn, bollyn.com, May 29, 2016

International Terrorism: The Propaganda War, Philip Paull, San Francisco State University, 1982

"Israeli Firm Loses N.Y. Airport Award," Charles R. Babcock,
Washington Post, April 12, 1987

"Israel in Afghanistan & Ehud Barak's $300 Million Rip-Off,"
Christopher Bollyn, bollyn.com, April 29, 2016

"Report: Netanyahu Says 9/11 Terror Attacks Good for Israel,"
Haaretz, April 16, 2008

Terrorism: How the West Can Win, Benjamin Netanyahu, Farrar
Straus & Giroux, 1986

The Zionist Plan for the Middle East, by Israel Shahak, a translation
of "A Strategy for Israel in the Nineteen Eighties" by Oded
Yinon, Association of Arab-American University Graduates,
Inc., Belmont, Massachusetts, 1982

U.S.-Pakistan Relationship: Soviet Invasion of Afghanistan,
A. Z. Hilali, Ashgate (U.K.) 2005

Wesley Clark speaking at the Commonwealth Club of California,
October 3, 2007, Fora.TV

"Why Did Iron Boil beneath the Rubble?" Christopher Bollyn,
bollyn.com, May 6, 2006

CHRISTOPHER BOLLYN is an investigative journalist and writer. After finishing high school in Schaumburg, Illinois, he sojourned in Europe and the Middle East before studying languages, history, and journalism at the University of California at Davis and Santa Cruz. He earned a degree in history with the focus on the Israeli occupation of

The author speaking to the Citizens' Grand Jury on the Crimes of 9-11 in Los Angeles, California, on October 23, 2004.

Palestine. After the first Gulf War he led an international team of photojournalists on a trip through the West Bank and Gaza Strip. He has written in-depth articles about the Middle East, electronic vote fraud, the dangers of depleted uranium, and the history and geo-political background of the terror attacks of 9-11. He has been invited to speak at numerous 9-11 events across Europe and the United States.

CPSIA information can be obtained
at www.ICGtesting.com
Printed in the USA
FSOW03n1706301017
40552FS